£1.50

CW01560346

Publishing Children's Poetry For 19 Years

Bust-A-Rhyme

Giving verse
a voice

Eastern England

Edited by Claire Tupholme & Donna Samworth

First published in Great Britain in 2010 by:

 Young**Writers**

Young Writers
Remus House
Coltsfoot Drive
Peterborough
PE2 9JX
Telephone: 01733 890066
Website: www.youngwriters.co.uk

Foreword

Young Writers' Bust-A-Rhyme competition is
a showcase for secondary school pupils to
share their poetic creativity and inspiration.
Selecting the poems has been challenging
and immensely rewarding. The effort and
imagination invested by these young writers
makes their poems a pleasure to enjoy
reading time and time again.

Young Writers was established in 1991 to
nurture creativity in our children and young
adults, to give them an interest in poetry and
an outlet to express themselves. Seeing their
work in print will encourage them to keep
writing and become our poets of tomorrow.

Contents

Kemnal Technology College, Sidcup

Pakefield Middle School, Pakefield

The Poems

London City In A Teenager's Head

Main town buildings of perfect Jimmy Choo's
The rivers the shade of eye shadow
Exactly baby-blue
The Gherkin no more but a slick brush of mascara
Pollution dressed as peach perfume
And cars into dazzling diamond tiara
Sunset is of a rosy-red blush
Prada handbags pinned with Lush
Green silk clothing grounded as grass
Laced roads carry French tags we watch them pass
Long fingers are branches which hold manicured nails
Our London Eye jewelled as a bright bangle
Every earring that has a dangle to each pair of prized sandal
This is our new generation London.

Naseema Khalique (13)

Different

Different is my name
Maybe I am just not the same
In the inside I am strong
You are just wrong

I am just alone
But I will not moan
I dread coming into school
Maybe I am just not cool

You always ruin my self-esteem
You always work as a team
Your words really hurt
Why are you so curt?

Let me live my life
I will not change
I am not ashamed of who I am
Be nice to me
Please!

Jessica Kate Worsley (12)
Babington House School, Chislehurst

The Point?

My smiles and 'I'm fines!'
are almost out of stock.
Days seem to carry on moving,
yet I feel like I go nowhere.

No one cares about me,
no one even notices me.
I sit there and see how happy
life would be, without me.

So what is the point of life?
'There isn't one!' I hear myself reply.
It's pointless.
Life's just so pointless!

No one sees beyond
my glazed-over eyes
which seem to be glued
to the view of the ground.

I wake up to a silence
and spend all day, every day
with no company but my own,
no acknowledgement from anyone.

So here goes,
my last ever post.
Yours truly,
      Miss Invisible.

Jessica Baker (13)
Babington House School, Chislehurst

Blamed!

I sit here all day
Lonely in my dark room
Wait, feeling blue,

Getting blamed is the only thing,
The thing my parents are good at,
All they can do is blame me!

My brother is kind and thoughtful
But every night he turns into this thing,
A dark, evil wolf,
He doesn't hurt me outside,
He hurts me inside with his dark nail-biting words.

And all they can do is blame me!

I was in a dark room
Full of black cats
So cuddly and cute
Leaned in to stroke it
Big mistake!
My foot hit the wall with a bang,
My parents screamed and shouted,
'Why must you do that?
Why?
Why?
Why?'

Sophie Prince (12)
Babington House School, Chislehurst

Words I Remember

Sticks and stones do hurt
But so do words far more
An ache or pain will fade in time
My soul is tender and sore.

Emerald eyes sear into my back
Spiteful words keep repeating in my head
Her vicious tongue twists and turns into words
Around they churn and mortify me.

They are directed like carving knives
Making wounds deep inside
I turn around, the lightning has struck again
How do I bide my time?

She is so cruel
I'm a fool to let it happen
What possible gain is there
To create such misery?

Word swords batter and break my self-esteem
Could she ever redeem herself by saying sorry?
No, she will move on and forget
But I will always remember.

Samantha Leighton (12)
Babington House School, Chislehurst

Goodbye

Nothing's going well right now,
My life is upside down;
Since that one day some weeks ago,
When I got some bad news.

I came home from school that day,
To find Daddy looking grim;
He told me to prepare myself
For something very, very sad.

He picked up the keys and climbed into the car
And so we drove and drove;
Past school and my friend's house,
Until we reached Saint John's Hospital.

We rushed inside the building,
Everybody looked at us with sorrow;
Then I realised what was going on
And that started to make me cry.

So there's a message to this poem,
Which is to respect your Mum;
And your dad and sisters and brothers,
You don't know when they'll disappear.

Aisling Murphy (13)
Babington House School, Chislehurst

The Wrong Place At The Wrong Time

As it was with Stanley in 'Holes',
Blamed for stealing shoes,
Banished to a desert camp,
Because they thought he was a scamp.

So it was with Tate's brother,
Walked from one place to another,
Not realising that little Madi had let one slip,
Was blamed for the pong,
When he did nothing wrong.

So it was with my sister
Who went to a party,
Tea with the Queen it was themed,
So she dressed up as a teapot, when all the others
Were dressed up like mothers.

So it was with my daddy,
Driving like crazy,
The officer out-ran him in their car
And found out he had skidded on the wet tar.

Alexandra Morton (11)
Babington House School, Chislehurst

Exam!

My fists were clenched with fear,
Sweat trickled down my face.
Exam day was here.

As they called us in,
My breathing became heavy.
How was I going to begin?

When I sat down on my chair
My head started screaming.
The pen just kept on stopping.
When I finished the test
My friends were all so fine.
I realised I could only do my best.

Antonia Thomlinson (13)
Babington House School, Chislehurst

Unlucky For Some
So it was with me
I drove to the airport one day
To find a guy sleeping on display
People walking up and down
And going all around.

It was so unlucky
That I was so mucky
Eating Kentucky.

I am on the phone
On the tarmac in pain
Sitting in the pouring rain
Wishing I was in Spain.

I was shopping in the Glades
To find myself in a daze
The lift got stuck at level two
It made me feel very blue.

Paige Brooks (11)
Babington House School, Chislehurst

The Coldness
On the train
With such vain
Watching the lion with his fluffy mane
Because of the coldness enclosing me

The storm is raging
The blizzard is ageing
My bones are aching
Because of the coldness enclosing me

Then the lion was awakening
Because he was shaking
By the earthquake rumbling
He roared and leaped, jumped onto the tumbling train
I snuggled up tight to my dad
Because of the coldness enclosing me.

Alex Green (11)
Babington House School, Chislehurst

The Wrong Place At The Wrong Time

So it was with me,
Watching X Factor and drinking tea,
When we heard something, *beep, beep, beep,*
My mum ran to the window, looked out,
The gate was open.
My dad pushed my mum out the way,
There was a man with a grey
Hoody and a bright torch.
My dad grabbed his bat,
Ran down the stair,
Straight to the door,
It was locked,
The robbers jumped jauntily over the fence.
We called the police that very night.

Charla Halil (11)
Babington House School, Chislehurst

Unlucky

So it was with my mum
Slipped on ice and fell with an almighty thump
Got up feeling rather embarrassed
And walked away harassed.

So it was when I was young
Went out shopping with my mum
Started hugging another lady
Ran to my mum feeling mortified
Started hugging her and cried.

So it was with my dad
Speeding down the road like mad
Got caught by the police
And all he wanted was some peace.

Maddison Trevor (12)
Babington House School, Chislehurst

The Weakest Link Kid

Every day I think about
What it's like to be appreciated,
It's like on 'The Weakest Link'
And I'm the one who's eliminated.

Punch, kick, flick, slap,
Every day I want to snap.

Walking up to me every day
With smiles on their faces,
Their behaviour really puts me down,
The disgrace is:
They're never sorry.

Daniela Russo (12)
Babington House School, Chislehurst

Food Is My Friend

They say they're my friends
I think of them as my friends
They call me fat
They're not my friends
Why can't they do it some other time?
My parents split up
I feel like it's my fault
I go to the shops
I buy some sweets
I eat them all
Food is my friend and enemy
It makes me feel better for a moment
Then I look down at my tummy
And I am appalled
I go to the loo with my toothbrush
And then throw up
I go to the kitchen
I am alone
I look at the knives.

William Ford (14)
Canterbury Steiner School, Chartham

I Am Who I Am Because Of You Guys

Anna
You know how to make me smile
Even from a mile
If anyone is ever mean, I can always lean on you.

Kizzy
When I am sad, I always talk to you
I swear your hugs are magic
You always take care of me when I am sad.

Ellie
Not many people know me like you do
I hope you know I love you too
When I cry you never make me feel bad.

Emma
You make me laugh even when I am crying
You always know when I am lying
You never judge me for being who I am.

Julia
You will always be my friend
You always lend a hand
You are so kind.

I am who I am because of you guys.

Scarlett Swain (15)
Canterbury Steiner School, Chartham

Living In Fear

Nowhere to hide
You are like a thorn in my side
You want to get me without fail
You've got such a nasty sting in your tail

You make fun of my size and the colour of my hair
You always leave me feeling stripped bare
I ask you what's wrong, so we can sort it out
But you get angry, nasty and shout

You are a bully
You don't like me, so you make me cry
It's not just the verbal and physical but the mental abuse
I have often thought about ending it, by putting my head in a noose

You're not strong, just aggressive and weak
You've never liked me because I'm kind and meek
My self-respect, you have taken away
But I hope and pray that it will come back someday

All that I really want is a friend
So I hope that all this will come to an end
My life feels like a battle that can never be won
All I want is to have some fun.

Annabelle Peppiatt (14)
Canterbury Steiner School, Chartham

Being Judged

His angry eyes met mine
As if I had committed a crime
Although after detention I thought
I'd done my time
Being judged is not too pleasant
His eyes half-closed like a moon that is crescent
I did not know what I had done
The amount of helplessness hit me like a ton
None of my friends offered assistance
I felt I was non-existent.

Robert Blackadder (14)
Canterbury Steiner School, Chartham

11

An Old Phrase Revised

A torn and bleeding mess she left
When sauntering away
From nothing really except me
Who just got in her way
I'm broken but I can't complain
Because what happens next
Numbs the pain in crippling ways
And shows her at her best
'You're worthless, devoid of a use
There's nowhere you belong.'
She needn't have said so though;
I've known it all along
So I put to you today
A renewing of the old
Sticks and stones may break bones
But words will shatter a soul.

Kizzy Amelia-Rose Millington (14)
Canterbury Steiner School, Chartham

Hell

They stare down like hawks
With their piercing eyes
In the corridor before class
Sniggering over their lies
In food tech it's the worst
Even though the teacher's looking
They push, knock and shove
When we're preparing cooking
But then we have lunch
And it's like feeding time at the zoo
I'm the small defenceless cub
They're the boxing kangaroo
Finally it's home time
And I think I've gotten away
Then they follow you home
And I sigh and wait for the next day.

Emma Ryan (14)
Canterbury Steiner School, Chartham

Different

He wouldn't walk out the house
Without a long flowing dress.
The many people of the city
Would stop and stare.
'You can't wear that! You're a boy!'
They would say.
He would walk on.
On the bus, on the tube
We could hear people
Whispering behind our backs
Pointing at the young boy
Wearing a dress.
He didn't care, until the age of seven
Then he noticed the whispering, pointing, staring
And never again, has he worn a dress.

Anna Caitlin Temple Roche (14)
Canterbury Steiner School, Chartham

Terribly Alone

Her angry eyes met mine,
With ringing and chimes,
The heart running and faltering,
As she hit with the wooden stick.
Her knees fell and she swelled
With the pulsing heart drumming.

No one is coming
Left all alone,
As she walks off with a superior stance.
As 'her' figure shrivelled in the corner
Weeping with shreds of tears.

Grace Tully-Fleming (14)
Canterbury Steiner School, Chartham

Crawling Home

She receives a slap as a welcome to school
They must think she is some sort of a fool
Her homework is taken and claimed as their own
And through it all there's not even a moan
She walks the miles back to her house
And stoops to pick up a half-dead mouse
Suddenly behind there is a shout,
'Look, it's the girl with the filthy snout,'
She turns with dread expecting the punch
And crawls her way home to finish the day.

Jessie Hanrath (14)
Canterbury Steiner School, Chartham

Angry Eyes

His angry eyes met mine
I looked up from writing a line
His face was purple with rage
I felt it was in a cage
He began to shout
I knew I was out
What had I done?
I wanted to run
I'd been judged unfairly
He had got lairy.

Peter Logan (14)
Canterbury Steiner School, Chartham

Best Friends

When we're playing together
As best friends,
It seems our fun
Will never end.
'Cause we're best friends
We'll stand up for each other,
The only people more special
Are our parents and brothers.

We're on our BMXs
Over jumps, round the track,
Or we're wrestling in the grass
Pinning each other on our backs.
We could be playing football
Scoring goals,
Or maybe at a party
Eating cakes and sausage rolls.
We might go to the beach
And swim in the sea,
Or watch a film at midnight
On our flatscreen TV.
If it started snowing
We'd have a snowball fight,
Or we could play snooker
All through the night.

But some days are not so fun
Our time is rough,
We'll be sitting in maths or history
With the teacher being tough.
Or if we've fallen out
And both are feeling miserable,
We'd need someone for comfort
To stop us feeling dismal.

When we're playing together
As best friends,
It seems our fun
Will never end.
'Cause we're best friends
We'll stand up for each other,
The only people more special
Are our parents or brothers.

Tom Borrett (12)
Claydon High School, Claydon

Mother Nature

You are like a summer's breeze, skipping through the trees,
With every step you take, you disturb the leaves,
You vanish like thin air, leaving not a hair,
For you are so real under fingertips.
Believed in by so many: sweet as you are
It's funny how one can fall in love with such little reason.
You believe in no violence, yet your world is bloody,
And when love hurts, my heart aches for you.
You douse the raging fire of pain, like snow
And once your voice has cried its last breath
I will be with you and will stop at no length,
Will run to your side in no time, not later.
My love will die not as the turn of nature
Though summer ends, I will be yours forever.

Amber-Rose MacKenzie (13)
Cornwallis Academy, Linton

What Is Laughing?

When I look up at the clouds,
I wonder what makes me laugh,
Is it a funny monkey
With arms so long it can reach the sky?
Is it a joke I hear from friends?
I laughed so hard my tummy hurts
And then I wonder if it is,
My grandad who is so funny too.
Now I think about it, I wonder what it is . . .
Could it be my sister, tickling me all day,
Or could it be my mummy giving me a cuddle?
But now as I look back on it I wonder if all these things,
Including you,
Will make me laugh for always.

Aimee Miller (11)
Cornwallis Academy, Linton

Sonnet

You take my heart and crush it to pieces;
Thy tender touch doth make me feel anew.
I can't love until my heart releases,
So why you make me feel the way I do?
Beauty far beyond the average human -
You use it to enthral me, every day,
It makes me think how no other man can -
Cheer me up when I am in such dismay.
Enchanting voice - I cannot get enough,
Though what I hear hurts me - they are cruel words.
You fool me into thinking this is love:
I think it is, my emotions have stirred.
Yet despite thy cruelness, I cannot bear
The way I do feel when you are not there.

Rosie Alexander-Pennie (12)
Cornwallis Academy, Linton

Friendship

Like as the sun shines over the blue day,
Your smile always fills me up with gladness,
My friendship with you will always climb high,
As it helps to wash away my sadness.
When we make each other laugh out loud
I am grateful that I have friends like you,
You make me feel amazingly proud,
There is never a day when I feel blue
And our friendship can stand the test of time,
There is nothing that can get in our way -
Without others we can get along just fine,
Friendship and life is a big game to play,
Yet we'll stick together through thick and thin,
Our hearts open, happiness flooding in.

Cara Brown (12)
Cornwallis Academy, Linton

Smile

My friend is a happy soul
Who makes me smile.
Helps me regain my happy style,
Will remain loyal through my life.
I met her sitting on a bench.
She wore a wide grin and stared at me,
Then I beamed back like a Cheshire cat.
She is my star in my sky,
Shining her brilliant smile.

Sophie Hewson (13)
Cornwallis Academy, Linton

Fun, Fun, Fun

Playgroup was like a dream
Where you can do anything you want,
The wooden climbing frame
And milk at 10 o'clock;
The toys, the friends and all the
Fun, fun, fun.

Class 1 is where you learn to read and write,
You also get to play
With the 'splash' of the water zone
Where everybody was,
The glittering golden sand
Falling gently between my fingertips at the sandpit.
Storytime and all the
Fun, fun, fun.

Class 3 is about World War I,
The River Nile
And growing up.
You act the role of a main part
In a boring play and
Wonder why the teacher is shouting
At you when you wake up.
You have strong friendships
And all the
Fun, fun, fun.

. . . And now here's me
With teenage dreams,
A good life I am living,
Parties, discos and all the
Fun, fun, fun.

Emily Pursehouse (13)
Diss High School, Diss

Paintball

Hiding in bunkers or behind walls,
Shooting the reds and watching them fall,
Splat goes the paintball, right next to my dad,
So I shoot down that player, he's out, he's dead,
If you hide they find you and attack,
But if you run, they drive you back.
Your friend stands up and next thing you know,
Splat! Straight in the head and out he goes,
You're the only one left, and they know where you are,
Paintballs flying over your head from afar,
You run straight out, towards their base,
But then you get shot, right in the face.
Splish, splash, splosh the sound of the mud,
Your feet are stuck, you're a sitting duck,
You're getting shot at, and then you get free,
Now you're angry, go on a shooting spree.
You throw the grenade, the one with the smoke,
Then you run through, trying not to choke,
You manage to touch their bunker, you won,
So to turn around, but you get shot in the bum.
It's the last round, you cannot get killed,
You just get hit, and carry on the thrills.
You grenade their bunker, get loads of kills,
You run out of paintballs and leaving time's here,
So you live, but you ache from ear to ear.

Jack Taylor (14)
Diss High School, Diss

FA Cup Final

He's running down the left,
It's the final play.
It's make or break,
To win the day!

He cuts in on his right,
This could be it.
He passes to the striker,
Swivel, hit!

He strikes the ball,
Clean and true.
With passion and hope
And power too!

It soars like a bird,
To the top.
Nobody can block it
Or make it stop!

It ripples the net
And cheers erupt.
'We've won, we've won
The FA Cup!'

Thomas Goddard (14)
Diss High School, Diss

Our Little Green Bench

Standing in the playground,
Listening to a funny sound,
Friends are telling stories,
But some are telling porkies,
Our little green bench,
Notre peu banc vert in French,
Stories about the teachers,
They are mean, mean creatures,
Without my friends where would I be?
Sitting on my own in the school canteen.

Lily Nunn (13)
Diss High School, Diss

My Memories

My memory as a little girl dressing up as a fairy princess
And the memory of posing on the trampoline, laughing, bouncing.
The memory of staining the carpet with my make-up set
And the memory of eating play dough with Yas, sneaking, hiding away.
My memory of visiting my dad's, sliding, riding down the bannister,
With tears rolling down my face as I crashed.
The memory of feeling grown up, adventuring out alone,
Flash. Snap. My memory caught on camera on holiday
And the noise of whistling, shouting as we pass boys.
The memory of summer, dressed for the sun,
Buying chips all day, spending hours at the park.
My memories of early hours in the morning with Stace,
The memories of sleepovers, how we laugh, scare and dare.
The memory of no sleep
And the strain of the next day.
My memory of screams as Chloe pulled back a strip,
The fear in Amy's eyes,
Followed by tears, not of pain, but laughter.

Bethany Driver (13)
Diss High School, Diss

It's My Dream

Travelling around the world, that's what I want to do,
Travel across the worldwide oceans, all crystal clear and blue.

Learning the cultures of many different places,
Making friends and seeing lots of faces.

Brazil, Japan and the Republic of Congo,
Only some of the places I want to go.

And I know at times I may miss home,
But deep inside I'll know I'm not alone.

The letters, the photos will forever be with me,
Think of all the places I am going to see.

Nothing will stop me because I'm so keen,
I will do anything to achieve my dream.

Bernadette Lovett (13)
Diss High School, Diss

Untitled

Just another individual,
Disguised as a smile.
Comes to meet you
But she doesn't know who you are.

She's pulling the puzzles apart,
Working out from A to B.
Take her back to the start,
Feelings are lost at sea.

Behind miles of windows and walls
A little girl on a broken swing.
Truth hits you like a lorry,
Mystery's a harmful thing.

She's been spending all her time
In a distant dreamy daze.
Individual disguised as a smile
Pulls the reins and gallops away.

Stacey Bartrum (13)
Diss High School, Diss

The Daring Days

Stupid, yet fun, each Saturday is new,
Too young but old enough.
We're crazy, we haven't got a clue.
We get 'the evils', people growl and stare,
Dirty looks in the street,
But we're young, we don't really care.
No real housework, just silly little jobs.
Empty the dishwasher, pick up your socks,
Sort out tiny bits and bobs,
Damaging, yet we get a puny social kick
Out of doing adult things.
Spending too much money, being sick.
So happy, each friend so caring,
Funny, trusting, gossiping and worry-free.
Being a teenager is great, so thrill-full and daring.

Yasmine Weale (13)
Diss High School, Diss

My Guardian Angel

The wind will whistle past you as you're falling through the air,
You feel as if you're flying, though you don't go anywhere.
But soon the wings grow from your back and take you to the skies,
Above the stars, the Earth, the moon, until you're flying high.

Float within the universe,
Burn within the light.
Don't hold it too tightly
Or you'll crush the butterfly.

A hand will find its way to yours and save you from the darts,
The angel who is by your side will leave a special mark.
Your troubles shared with one another in a million ways
And now you're here together you can make it through the haze.

Float within the universe,
Burn within the light.
Don't hold it too tightly
Or you'll crush the butterfly.

Charlotte Mann (13)
Diss High School, Diss

In 10 Years Time . . .

In 10 years time where will I be?
Living in a mansion or living by a tree?
Will I be with Mr Right
Or getting paid to have a fight?
Will I live like the Queen
Or still dress like a stroppy teen?
Will I have the perfect job
Or be working for a slob?
Will I be a celebrity
Or be known as Doggy?
Will I be called a loving wife
Or be trying to work out life?
Wherever I am,
I'm sure I'll find the perfect man.

Agnes Fitzpatrick (13)
Diss High School, Diss

Without Friends

Without friends I would be a baby with no smile,
Without friends my life would be miserable.
Without friends where would the good times be
And all the memories where would they be?

Without friends there would be no happy,
Without friends I wouldn't share my secrets.
Without friends I wouldn't laugh,
Without friends where would I be on the life path?

Without friends I would feel all selfish,
Without friends I wouldn't share.
Without friends I would feel very lonely
And I would turn all moany . . .

. . . Without friends I would be lost at sea,
Without friends I would have no future.
Without friends there would be no shopping sprees
And I would always feel guilty, especially towards me.

Rebecca Jones (13)
Diss High School, Diss

Paintball Madness

Splat! It has begun already,
Paintballs zooming at 200mph.
Me and my best mate Ali, me and him, our own squad.
We work like a perfect team.

Zwang! There goes my flash grenade,
Bang! There goes Ali's paint grenade,
Then we see three of their team leave the arena,
But me and Ali realise we are the last ones left!

We are taking lots of fire.
Then the whistle blows, it's over but we aren't hit,
It is one of our team, he captures the flag.
He must have camped back,
But still four more rounds to go . . .

Kieran Rush (13)
Diss High School, Diss

Always There

Always there waiting for you to get home from school
Always there wagging his tail
Always there to cheer you up when you're feeling down
Always there to play with
Always there to make you smile
Always there to listen without interrupting
Always there to teach new tricks
Always there to protect you
Always there to eat your homework
Always there to make you laugh
Always there through good and bad
Always there through thick and thin
Always there, always hungry
Always there to hug
Always there to love
Without him I'd be lost
I love my dog.

Rosie Chubbock (13)
Diss High School, Diss

When I'm Older

When I'm older I want to travel the world,
See Africa, Antarctica and Egypt.
I want to visit Pompeii, see the ruins,
To bungee-jump off bridges and dive off cliffs.

When I'm older I want to go into space,
Walk on the moon and visit Mars.
Gaze at the stars, the planets and moon,
Discover new planets and discover new life.

When I'm older I want to be rich,
To own a mansion and thousands of clothes.
I want lots of nice cars and a designer dog,
With lots of friends and lots of shoes.

When I'm older I want a lot,
But most of all I just want to be me.

Sophie Chittock (14)
Diss High School, Diss

Stereotypes

Just because we're teenagers
It doesn't mean we have no soul.
We're human beings just as much as you,
It's just because we're a younger age.
We have dreams in our sleep the same as you
And we dream about normal things too.
Although the news will hit you like a rock,
It's entirely true.
People today are stereotypical about us, it's just we get fed up.
People blame us for everything, but older people do it too.
Everyone is so shocked at a teenage stabbing
And yet other ages do the same.
If adults stop acting like they do, we would have an example
And stop it too.
It's time we should make our stand, we can be as good as gold
But with all sorts of stereotypes trying to flatten us,
How can we give it a go?

Tristan Stanforth (13)
Diss High School, Diss

Glory Of The Sun

To bask in the glory of the sun
Feels wonderful on a summer's day,
It gives you the energy to laugh, sing and play,
It makes you want to dance around
And jump high off the ground,
The rustling sound of the trees
Dancing around in the summer breeze,
The warmth of the sleepy summer air
As you sit on your comfy deckchair,
It makes you feel so very good
As if you really, really could
Do anything you wanted to.
I don't know; it's up to you.

Robert Payne (13)
Diss High School, Diss

My Dog

He barks,
He bites,
He's playful,
He's nice,
He's a bully,
He's a thief,
He's a friend.

He's a lion and a teddy bear,
Who hunts for shoes to eat,
He's a monster and an athlete,
Whose life revolves around meat.

He loves every human being
And hates them all as well
And even though he's an animal,
Is he really that different from us?

William Ransom (13)
Diss High School, Diss

Best Friends

We played princesses together at nursery,
We were mums to our baby dolls,
We made play dough cookies at playschool,
We walked through the scary school gates together.
Being little was simple and fun, but we wanted to be 'big girls'.
Now we're the 'big girls' we wanted to be,
It's not that bad, but we miss being young and carefree.
We still have each other and that helps so much.
We tell each other everything,
We laugh at each other a lot.
We spend every weekend together.
We will always be there for each other,
This is all because we were, we are and always will be best friends.

Danielle Clark (13)
Diss High School, Diss

Because We're Friends

We laugh like hyenas at all the inside jokes,
We do this because we're friends.

We chuckle at the pictures we took many moons ago,
We do this because we're friends.

We giggle in class and we just can't stop,
We do this because we're friends.

We snicker at the weird and wacky 'hot new' trends,
We do this because we're friends.

And I know we'll stay friends
Until the very, very end.

Polly Stammers (13)
Diss High School, Diss

I Am Strong

I am strong because I turned down drugs.
I am strong because I turned down the temptation of alcohol.
I am strong because I stood up to the bullies.
I am strong because I fought the pressure from a boy.

I'm a tough cookie so accept that's the way I am.

I am strong because I didn't steal money for transport to a party.
I am strong because I can behave when others around me don't.
I am strong because I'm not afraid to stand up for what I believe in.
I am strong because I don't care what other people think.

I am a tough cookie so accept that's the way I am.

Abi Joy (13)
Diss High School, Diss

Like Lego

They make me laugh until my stomach aches,
My eyes water and my jaw breaks.
I've never known people just quite like them,
They bring joy to my life again and again.
When I'm out with my family it's just not the same,
To be honest I find it completely lame.
For they don't take stupid pictures until there's no memory,
Try on dresses, chat for hours or go hyper and silly.
We click like Lego, we're the latest trends,
I don't know how I could live without my friends.

Jemma Clark (14)
Diss High School, Diss

School!

Things I love about school are . . .
The children laughing like hyenas.
The kids running around the playground like a herd of elephants.
The classrooms being bright and colourful like a sweet shop.
The jokes and laughs filling the school to bursting point.
Being with friends and sharing our secrets, whisper, whisper.
The teachers helping you with your work
And helping us leave our childhood behind.
So my ambition is to be a teacher.

Natalie Leeder (13)
Diss High School, Diss

Get Out Of Bed!

Oh no! Oh no!
The door opens.
'Wakey, wakey! Time to get up now.'
Oh no!
The light shining in my eyes
Trying to get up but . . .
I just can't.
The clock ticking.
The nice, furry pillow getting pulled away
By June our morning waker.
Oh no, oh no!
Help! My pillow falling on my face.
My duvet's so warm, don't take it away!
Oh no, oh no, help me!
All these years getting up at the crack of dawn
I just need a break.
Oh, please help me!
Please let me stay in this soft, warm bed!
Please, just please, give me a break!

Gabriel Monks (12)
East Court School for Dyslexia, Ramsgate

Oh TV!

What brilliant channels you have
They are just so outstanding
I could watch you all day
TV, you are so excellent
So good
Oh no!
Here's Mum!
Oh no! Oh no!
I've got to turn it off
Oh please, now I'm sad
I'm upset
I'm missing my favourite programme
Oh well. It's time for the football match!

Oscar William Phillips (12)
East Court School for Dyslexia, Ramsgate

31

I hate You, Maths!

Maths, stupid maths
You stink like a pig
That smells like new Lynx
I'd rather go home and knit with my nan
And make pompoms the size of the sun
I wish I could shout
In the middle of the class
'I hate you, maths!'
I might as well pass.

Sam Neil (11)
East Court School for Dyslexia, Ramsgate

Don't You Hate Them?

Don't you hate them?
The spineless monsters
That seek out the shiniest
Of people to taunt and tease,
The bullies that terrorise quieter people
And frighten them.

Don't you hate them?
The cause of the hurt and confused,
The evil predator and the poor prey,
The victim of the bully's fun,
The people that steal
The little self-esteem they have left
And shatter it into pieces.

Don't you hate them?
The ones that cause
Depression, misery and pain,
That makes their victim
Believe there is no escape
And that they are the weaker ones,
The bullies that destroy any hope
With their verbal punches.

Don't you hate them?

Olivia Bayfield (12)
Flegg High School, Martham

The Death Of A Loved Relative

I have a bad feeling,
Something isn't right . . .
I get this feeling in my bones;
My chest tenses very tight.

I have a bad feeling,
Ring, ring . . . ring, ring . . .
There goes the telephone;
The news that it will bring.

I have a bad feeling,
I feel so afraid . . .
The terrible news I cannot take;
The destruction it has made.

I have a bad feeling,
I feel so down.
As though all the happiness drained out of me;
I feel as sad as a clown.

I have a good feeling,
They're at peace and at rest . . .
The sun shines soundless shimmering;
As it sets restless in the west.

I have a good feeling,
They are at harmony . . .
Elated in Heaven;
Thinking about all the memories.

I have a good feeling,
Even though I am still sad . . .
I think of all the good times;
It makes me feel less bad.

I have a good feeling,
All the pain will cease . . .
I am happy if they are too;
They'll be at a tranquil peace!

Amy Graves (12)
Flegg High School, Martham

Nobody Knows

Why am I not loved?
I always get pushed and shoved.
I'd give anything to have a friend,
I wish I didn't have to pretend,
As far as my life goes,
Nobody knows.

When Mum dropped me off here that day,
I didn't know what to say.
Ever since she drove off with that man,
I've been waiting here eating cold beans from a can.
As far as my life goes,
Nobody knows.

The only form of company that I seem to get,
Are the birds that twitter and the ladybird I once met.
The night and day seem so far apart,
And I just sit here with a broken heart.
As far as my life goes,
Nobody knows.

At night I wander around in the dark,
With the sound of cats screeching and loud dogs that bark.
Cold and scared I huddle in the gutter,
The people that pass me just stare and then mutter.
As far as my life goes,
Nobody knows.

I wish someone would take me from this nightmare,
Why has my life turned out like this?
It's just not fair.
During the day I wander around the street,
Looking in the bins for something to eat,
As far as my life goes,
Nobody knows.

One day a kind lady sat down to talk,
After a while we went for a walk.
We came to a stop outside a big door,
I thought to myself, *why? What for?*
As far as my life goes,
Nobody knows.

Before I knew it,
I was cosy in a bed,
Warm and clean and very well fed
With a new family who really cared,
No more reason to be lonely and scared.
As far as my life goes,
Nobody knows. (But they did!)

Paige Chloe Dyble (13)
Flegg High School, Martham

Child Abuse And Poverty

Every child has a right to life,
To love and help and care,
To some loving parents,
Of which some are never there.

Some children live in poverty,
Some children are abused,
Sometimes it's the parents fault,
But the kids are always accused.

Some people try to help them,
But the kids don't understand
They're not there to hurt them
They're there to lend a hand.

Some children live in wonder
Paralysed with fear
To take on all the wretched abuse
And not even shed a tear.

Of all the things that hurt you
Nothing can compare
To all the hurt those children get
Instead of parents to care.

Although we may not think it
It is very well true
We may be in a recession
But these kids aren't as lucky as you.

Jessica Hilton (13)
Flegg High School, Martham

The Rat

Crawling, a strong smell enveloped the grimy air
And the sun shone through the manholes
The scuttling of a creature in the distance

A grotesque face, teeth like knives piercing any being
Torturing the eye
Tail like a whip, long and thin
In the distance

A coarse hide dark as the night
Caught the sun as the creature darted through the segment of light
Portraying down a slight glimpse of the outside world

The secretive appearance of this creature rattles your bones
And sends shivers down your spine
It is a terrifying sight to behold as the beguiling eyes hunt you down

Emerging from its dark lair
And into the open
Among the shrubs - food in sight
Scuttling over - taking the first bite

Trapped
People coming over
Masks - tubes
The man's person read extermination

The creature cowered in the corner
In the shadows
Its purpose unknown
The carcass lay in peace - the plague had gone
Trapped forever . . .

Oliver Barker (13)
Flegg High School, Martham

Orphan

I sit and wait
Staring at the clock. It's hands seem to move
Backwards, just to spite me . . .
Each slow, steady tick-tock sounding like rhythmatic laughter.

They should be home by now,
I stare at the phone, willing it to ring.
To pick it up, and hear that it's all OK,
And that they're just running late.
Very late.

The phone rings.
The policeman. The car crash. the time of death.
The meaningless condolences . . .
What's the point? They're not coming back.

I see them everywhere.
On the bus, at school, walking past me
Hand in hand.
But I blink and they're gone . . .

I am alone
Nobody to stop my tears; or to hold my hand.
I am vulnerable.
Nobody to pick me up when I fall or make it all better . . .

I am an orphan . . .

Harriett Douglas (13)
Flegg High School, Martham

Drowning Nightmares

My eyes flutter stupidly shut, the nightmares begin,
The annoying, the frustrating, the depressing sins.
Sometimes I fall, sometimes I drown
And when I awake I'm bearing a frown,
But it's not always me, sometimes there are others
Whether they be friends, relations or mothers.
They happen so differently, they pain and devour,
But lucky for me they last no more than an hour,
Then I awake screaming and crying,
I run to my mum, she says they're just lying.
But I struggle to calm, they promised they'd get me
And I can't shake the feeling of falling so painfully,
Under the water my lungs burn,
Above the water I toss and turn,
Through the clouds I fall down,
Struggling to decide if I'd rather drown,
Men chase me guns in their arms
And their shouts promise to do me harm,
Then I fall dead of heat and thirst,
Sometimes I feel like I've been cursed,
Now I realise that this is not the truth
And I really am disappearing as fast as my youth.
I am drowning, falling not exactly fun
But at least peace has finally come.

Dearna Johnson (12)
Flegg High School, Martham

Waiting

I trudged along the dusty path
And stared up the road ahead.
I wander these streets every day,
Just waiting, waiting.

My legs all scratched,
My elbows bruised,
I wait for someone to come,
Just waiting, waiting.

I watch all the children,
Laughing and playing,
Wishing it was me,
Just waiting, waiting.

I wish I had nice clothes
And nice food and a home.
I wish I had someone
And not be alone,
Just waiting, waiting.

To this day I wait,
For someone to find me,
Just waiting, waiting
For someone to come.

Emma Walford (13) & Emily Sellick (12)
Flegg High School, Martham

A Girl's Life

All the secrets
All the lies
The flaming fury
In your eyes

All the snogging
All the pain
Teardrops fall
You did it again

All the support
All the hate
Best friends by your side
We will never separate

All the fighting
All the betrayal
As the bullies push and shove
You're left bruised, very fragile

All the cheating
All the noise
There's only one thing
It can be: *boys!*

Abigail Ransome & Emma Barwood (12)
Flegg High School, Martham

A Healthy Poem

Skating on the rink,
Gliding happily along,
Eating healthy food.

Sprinting excitedly,
Without a care in the world,
Eating healthy food.

Loving fruit and veg,
I'm keeping fit and healthy,
Eating healthy food.

Olivia Mercer (12)
Flegg High School, Martham

The Silent Battle

It had been hard to see,
In the blinding sun,
But I still blamed me,
For the battle that had begun.

I stared down at his beautiful face,
My little angel in disguise,
He will soon be in a better place,
Where he can't hear my cries.

Every breath is a grain of sand in an hourglass,
Constantly counting down the time,
I inhale allowing it to pass,
It feels like a terrible crime.

His skin too pale against the white,
Of these hospital walls,
He's edging closer to eternal night,
With every tear that falls.

Then the nurse walks slowly by
And looks at my wonderful son,
She announces with a sigh,
That death has finally won.

Lucie Rose Barber (13)
Flegg High School, Martham

Always Be Here

I walk down the corridor, alone, alone
I walk to my classroom, alone, alone
I enter my lesson, they're there, they're there
I have a fear they'll always be there

They look over at me, I'm scared, so scared
They walk over by me, I'm scared, so scared
They lean over to say, they say, they say
We will always be here

I go to the playground, afraid, afraid
I open my lunchbox afraid
I turn round and see, they're there, they're there
They always stay true to their word

They sit next to me, I stop breathing, I freeze
I tremble, I shake, I go weak at the knees
'Please don't hurt me,' but they do as they please
Crash, bang, wallop, bruise.

I walk into school in pain, in pain
I walk to my lesson in pain, in pain
I turn right around surprised, surprised
They are no longer here.

Jack Mayhew-Stone (12)
Flegg High School, Martham

42

Wake In The Night

Waking to the darkness of the daring night,
With the screams of black terror,
Scrambling to my feet,
Creeping silently to the open window.

Straining my tired eyes,
I tried to make sense of the commotion,
Slowly piecing together the faint glow
Of an evil white cross.

My heart pounding with frightening fear,
I turn to the old, oak door,
Seeing someone's dark silhouette,
Turn and creep across the hall.

As I reach the porch,
I hear the sound of rubbery tyres,
Reversing off the gravel,
Into the blackness of the night . . .

Sliding back into bed,
With the calming sound of silence,
I drift into a deep sleep.

Jade Avery & Beth Fielding (12)
Flegg High School, Martham

Dancing Bear

The day goes by very slowly
As I do tricks and roly-polys
Somersaults, jumps, I feel ill
I want to eat or make a kill

I'm all worn out, I try to give up
But if I do he'll pull me up
My boring life is really grim
My owner wouldn't like it if it was him

If I'm hungry and I try to attack
My owner will hit me whack, whack, whack
No one hears my bear-like cries
Or see my tears come from my eyes

My mouth is chained, my legs are breaking
Every day my owner's taking
Through the year and through the day
I very slowly pass away.

Molly Draba-Mann (12)
Flegg High School, Martham

The Creepy Dream

One night, I came home from the store
And came across a large crooked door,
The house towered above me like a pile of stones
And the roof looked like some tattered bones.
I went through the door to see what was there
And I got quite a shock,
When standing there on the flight of stairs,
Was a great big hairy clock.
He stared at me with his great 9 and 3, and said, 'Get outta my house,'
I turned to him and said right back, 'Hey, that's a pretty pink blouse.'
He ran away back up the stairs and I heard the door slam shut,
I ran upstairs to find the clock, then I fell, now I'm cut.
Soon I found him in his room and someone with a gun,
I looked at it and screamed, 'Oh no, it's a Greggs sticky bun.'

Harry Wright & Josh McNe (12)
Flegg High School, Martham

Love, Life And Death

28th day, 28th day
A day of new life,
New life, a blossoming flower;
To reunite families,
Destroyed by lies.

29th day, 29th day,
A day of love and joy,
As new life flourishes;
In the serenity of a loving family,
Reunited by the flower of life.

30th day, 30th day,
A day of death and sorrow,
Families left devastated;
By the sudden death of the flower,
Taken into death's embrace.

Jed Prudames (12)
Flegg High School, Martham

The Big, Scary Monster

The big, scary monster - was big, was scary
But I was wary of the scary monster I named Hairy Warey

The bold, ugly monster - was bold, was really ugly
He was told that he was old and smelt of mouldy mould

The dumb, stupid monster - was dumb, was stupid
I bit his thumb and bum and gum,
He cried and sucked his thumb

The big, scary monster - was big, was scary
But Hairy Warey did not scare me because he wasn't there

The shy, friendly monster - was shy, was friendly
I was glad bad, sad monster had turned a new leaf

The cool, happy monster - now my cool, happy friend
Was the friendliest monster ever who is here to stay, hooray!

Jack Salter (13)
Flegg High School, Martham

Dogs

Dogs, dogs, dogs
Those cute little dogs
Those excited dogs
Bouncing through the meadow

Those female dogs
Male dogs
Large dogs
Small dogs
Doesn't matter to me

I've seen many dogs
Heard many dogs
Those memories we shared
Those heart-warming dogs.

Chelsea Nichols (12)
Flegg High School, Martham

Skateboarding

S kateboarding is really fun
K ick-flips are easy to do
A rti Au Sari has the nicest kick-flips
T re Flips are fun too
E very skating trick looks cool
B ails are where you fall off
O llies are where the board comes off the ground
A irs look cool over Goths
R ock to fakies look 'steezy'
D riveways are fun to ride
I ndys is where you grab the board
N ollies are fun to try
G rinds are where your trucks slide.

Oscar Bews-Miller (12)
Flegg High School, Martham

Sekigahara

Two armies collide at Sekigahara, central Japan.
The largest battle fought on Japanese soil.
A sword, a bow and a cannon, assigned to every man.
A colossal cauldron of darkness and turmoil.
The Samurai elite are ready, lives willing to take,
Ieyasu consults his advisors, what a hero he will make.
The battle begins and the armies advance.
The western force brandish their arms, the eastern enter a trance.
With a lightning flash the cavalry charge, the horses tread the sod,
While Mitsunari remains at large.
When the smoke has cleared, and all is destroyed but man,
Ieyasu, cheers he has achieved his mission
To unify all of Japan.

Joe Isaacs & Cameron Roote-Low (13)
Flegg High School, Martham

The Love You Save

Step by step, second by second,
I felt my heart smash into one thousand shimmering pieces.
Step by step, second by second,
I saw my only true love, march into the jaws of Hell.

This could be the last time we meet, my love,
So I run up to kiss him, and feel him kiss back,
This could be the last time we kiss, my love,
Tears fill both our eyes.

You have to move on, be brave, be strong
And save all your love for me.
While I am away, my heart is all yours,
Yours and yours only to be.

When we meet again, we will reunite,
Like two robins who have found each other,
After many a day of searching.
But as we drift further and further apart,
You must know, with all my heart, my love,
Nothing can come between us. Never. Ever.

Emily Compton (13)
Hayes Secondary School, Hayes

The Can Says

The can says 'sparkling low calorie soft drink',
But to me it's so much more,
It's a breeze on a warm summer's day,
The laughter of a friend.

The sweet, cool liquid, 'best served ice-cold',
How could you have it any other way?
It's the taste of long ago summers,
Unearthed memories from forgotten times.

The low hiss of the can crack open,
I can hardly keep back a grin,
As I am submerged in the euphoria,
Diet Coke - it's refreshing and sugar free!

In some ways it is like a drug,
You just can't keep away,
As the sweet bubbles paralyse your senses,
You don't get this from any other drink.

With a library of flavours,
You just can't say no,
Cherry, lemon, vanilla, lime
With each comes the same sugar-fuelled thrill.

The joy that comes with drinking Coke,
The sensation of great bliss,
There are some things in life you just can't describe,
And Coke is one of these.

Coke is like a sudden light,
Being turned on in the dark.
Once you have it, you never know
How you got on without.

Its reputation precedes it, no more needs to be said,
Coke: the first,
The original,
The sweetest,
Most popular,
The best.

Megan Elizabeth Cardy (13)
Hayes Secondary School, Hayes

Remember Me

I see my life flash before my eyes
I see my friends weeping in sorrow.

I see my family say, 'Why him, God why him?'
I see the light with God's hands.

I go through the light and in there
There is my nanny waiting for me.

I see her face, I see her smile
I cuddle her with lots of emotion.

I am united with her, with family and friends
With hugs and kisses forever and ever.

I have my moments thinking, *why am I here?*
I've fought my country but I've killed people.

Why am I in Heaven?
Why not in Hell?
Who took my life?
Did someone take theirs?

So from now I watch my family
Help them through life until they are here.

Will it be soon?
Will it be never?
When will they die?
And how?

I love my family lots and I'll never stop loving them
I am grateful for them loving me but I hope that they can see.

I want them to live their life instead of grieving me
I love them all so much
They mean the world to me.

Becky Nicole Jones (14)
Hayes Secondary School, Hayes

A Poppy

Among the dead bodies, caught in the crossfire
And the remains of shelter,
Nothing but bits, I see nothing but a poppy, a peaceful, red poppy.

Even faced with your friend with a gun to his head
And the dream of children running towards you
Congratulating you with your victory.
I see nothing but a poppy, a peaceful red poppy.

When you get clapped and recognised,
Wished luck,
I see nothing but a poppy, a peaceful red poppy.

In those nightmares of the frontline and the deaths,
I see nothing but a poppy, a peaceful red poppy.

You see this is all a lie,
There's more than what meets the eye.
This is what I tell myself, what I reassure myself,
Because when I close my eyes I see nothing but death and destruction.
So I imagine a poppy, a peaceful red poppy.

Endless nights I toss and turn,
Watching soldiers choke and burn.
I lay as my wife cuddles me
And remember those with such determination that weren't so lucky.
A poppy is a poppy, a dream is a dream
But a war is something no one wants to see.

So I close my eyes and squeeze them tight,
Then tell myself I'll be alright.
That's all, that's all inside my head,
A poppy, a peaceful red poppy.

Danielle Murphy (13)
Hayes Secondary School, Hayes

Gallop To Death

I could see them coming at me,
Guns and weapons at the ready.
Dead bodies flung right off their horses,
At least my man was still holding on steady.

Smack! Another horse had crashed in my side,
I thought I was gone forever.
My front legs were in pain but I could not stop,
Not now, not later, never.

I couldn't see what may be ahead,
Other horses surround me.
At least I will die brave and noble,
Helping fight for my country that is she.

Bang! Yet another shot was fired,
It was louder than ever before.
I knew it was closer, closest it could be,
Suddenly I could not fight anymore.

One leg collapsed then the other,
In my leg the bullet went.
I was in so much pain, too much to handle,
Brave and noble? This is not what I meant.

I got more tired and I could not see,
But still my rider pushed me on.
I needed to stop, the pain was sickening,
I was going, going, gone.

Olivia Ann Harris (13)
Hayes Secondary School, Hayes

Postcard From 37

Dusty long roads
Ones upon I used to stride,
A fiery furnace
And the shadows in which I used to hide.

Olive trees and branches
The fierce winds that used to blow,
The rain that fell
And the puddles the sun refused to show.

The breezy walks home
The laughter, the friends, the smiles,
Not anywhere near now
Just a distance of miles and miles.

Dust clouds and sandstorms
And the darker nights that followed,
Fragments of the past
Like a tree long ago been hollowed.

The steps to the black door
The number 37,
The sympathetic smiles to implore
That 'home' was no longer heaven.

Dina Rider (13)
Hayes Secondary School, Hayes

I Am A Rabbit

I am a rabbit who lives in a hutch,
And I don't like it very much.
There's nothing to do and nothing to see,
There are so many places I would rather be.

People stand there through the wires and stare,
It is as if they don't really care.
I feel so lonely it is not fair,
But it's better than being out there.

I have got toys,
But they make too much noise.
I also have water and plenty of food,
But it is still not too good.

I guess I am just a rabbit in a hutch,
And I still don't like it very much.

Victoria Janes (11)
Hayes Secondary School, Hayes

Fading Away

I walk along the road of dust,
Today I leave, I know I must.
But everything I leave behind,
When I return I will not find.
There's one more thing I must do,
Choose what to take, it's nothing new.
This war's been going on for ages,
My diary has too many pages.
But now it's time to say goodbye,
I want to leave this place on a high.
But somehow I just can't help thinking,
My home country is slowly sinking.
The sound of guns,
The commander talking,
Fading, fading away.

Jessica Maguire (13)
Hayes Secondary School, Hayes

A World Of Words

A world of words on pages marked in ink,
A blurb to tell you all you need to know without spoiling the end,
A front cover which pulls you in, makes you want to open it up and read.
Something so small with the ability to lose a person of any size,
Maybe not as exciting as the telly or as interesting as music,
But can thrill, scare or make you cry, all emotions and feelings,
With fiction and facts, a storyline,
Can make you see love, life or just a sad tale,
Inspire dreams or a poem, can make you see life in a whole new way.
To never enjoy a book or get lost in the story,
Is such a shame.
If only I could show you,
Let you into this world, where you don't need pictures to see,
A book is all you need.

Kate Rose Mawbey (14)
Hayes Secondary School, Hayes

Autumn

I'm four years old
And I'm in autumn.
I feel the crunch of crumpled leaves,
Swishing on my new red wellington boots.
I smell the fresh air
And the spook of Hallowe'en.
The fresh cut smile of *boo!*
The sound of *bang, bang, bang!*
For the fireworks and the bonfire,
The *crash, crack and swish,*
Colours of rainbows, spark of silver and gold
And the sight of the beautiful light,
In autumn,
In autumn.

Kerry Natalie Walker (11)
Hayes Secondary School, Hayes

War!

I woke up to sirens,
The smell of blood stained the air.
Telling me a nightmare,
Hearing whining noises of the bombs as they fell.
It was a hard story to tell.

My mum ran into my room and grabbed my hand,
Tugging me along as she ran.
Lights emerging from the black,
Leading us both to a bunch of sand sacks.

Soldiers running into our space
And tears of fear running down my face.
War is violent, upsetting, terrifying and forceful.

Alexander Vincent O'Connor (12)
Hayes Secondary School, Hayes

There's Guilt At The End Of Bad Journeys

The spitefulness, horridness, the hurtful comments they say,
I walk ahead, I turn around,
they just won't go away,
a blanket full of mist covering the sun,
before the Rainbow Nation
some people then wanted to be one.

The anger, the revenge - you can't step up to it.
It's not the way you look or act,
it's the way you really feel,
deep in your memories the bad things are never sealed.

You try to look as if you don't care,
you close your eyes and open them to imagine they weren't there.
You suddenly become a shadow, you no longer have control,
when a bunch of tears come exploding out you could not hold.

The relief then comes you've got your emotions out of there,
people realise you're not made of steel,
when they realise you had enough and can now stick up for yourself,
they begin to get guilt no matter how they felt.

Aisha Aldris (12)
Hethersett High School, Hethersett

Head To Wind

Ready, sitting in the boat,
Five minute bells about to go,
Looking for the wind's direction,
The tell-tales are showing east.

I set off towards the start line,
Two minutes has just passed,
So many boats out on the glistening water,
But my Tera's going to win.

I'm sailing on the mark now,
The winds are picking up,
Going to be some healing out there,
It's going to be great.

Finally the bell has gone,
The race has just begun,
I'm going head to wind,
Gonna have to tack.

Now going round the mark,
The boat's about to tip,
Leaning right out the boat,
Heart racing, energising, breathtaking.

Picking up some speed now,
Listening to the water rushing along the hull,
Boat jumping over waves like kangaroos under the sun,
Yes, I've taken over someone,
Three more boats to beat.

Just gone past another mark,
Only one more mark to go,
The wind has just died down, I'm going on a reach,
Pull the centre board up, yes I'm away.

Someone's in my way now,
I'm on starboard, excellent,
I have right of way,
Only one more boat to beat then victory.

Just witnessed someone capsize,
Their world's turned upside down,
Jumping on the centreboard,
The boats now ready to go.

Racing towards the line now,
I'm right behind the splash,
I take a sneaky tack and cross the line,
Yes! I've won, cheering as I sail back.

Now, arrived back on the pontoon,
Getting congratulations,
Going to get a trophy and medal,
Awesome, immense, thrilling.

Megan Laura Smith (13)
Hethersett High School, Hethersett

Grandad

I enjoyed every moment with you,
It's so sad that you had to go,
I miss your love, hugs and kisses,
I just wanted to let you know.

You made my nanny so happy,
you were a great grandad to me,
I wish you were still here,
you made our family complete.

The way you played with all four dogs,
you made it so much fun,
you had so much love to give,
and saw good in everyone.

Save a place for Nanny,
for when her time comes,
in the meantime we will take care of her,
because we know she's your number one.

So sleep tight Grandad,
our love for you will never end,
but as each day passes by,
our broken hearts will mend.

Courtney Radley (12)
Hethersett High School, Hethersett

PKC And Me

I am very different
in a way I can't explain
I don't know anybody else
who can share my pain.

It all builds up inside
emotions driving me
to feel alone in this place
a place I shouldn't be.

Sometimes I get so angry
that I just break down and cry
sometimes I want to tell the world
because my life is one big lie.

It makes all I do harder
and I can't speak up and say
that this thing possessing me
is making things this way.

But I look out at the rest of you
wondering, *what will be . . . ?*
Will I get a job? Drive a car?
See all I want to see.

Why can't I be accepted?
Why can't people see through?
See underneath this illness
and know I'm like the rest of you.

I promise you it won't beat me
live with it I may
but I'll carry on with my life
living day by day . . .

Paige Staff (12)
Hethersett High School, Hethersett

58

Dusk

My footsteps echo on the path, dusty and plain,
it ran through the park,
once filled with laughter and happiness,
now lifeless barren almost.
Echoes of children's laughter rang in my ears,
ghosts of happier times.
As I walk, the wind blew me back, forcing me out of this place,
leaves hopping into it and smashing into me like jets.
They continued on behind me,
trying to get away like everything I ever loved and cherished.
Travelling to a happier place.
Thoughts swept into my head, like the wind trying to cause me further pain.
When? My perfect song ending perhaps too quickly.
A box around my head, hiding my shame and disgrace,
while not letting any light in.
A tear ran down my cheek.
I found a crooked bench and sat.
An old swing, it was moving slightly, making me uneasy,
my life had fallen apart like paper in the rain.
When has it gotten so dark? Dusk had wormed its way into the twilight sky
like a ninja.
I got up and began to leave.
Footsteps slow and clumsy, almost cautious.
How had this all happened?
It was so quick yet so slow, so bumpy and so smooth.
So beautiful and so ugly, so happy and so sad.
It had been the worst day of my life.

Liam Forkes (12)
Hethersett High School, Hethersett

In The Night . . .

In the night I walk the streets
In the night I search for prey
In the night you better run
In the night - well I'm your worst nightmare.

Josh Thompson (14)
Hethersett High School, Hethersett

Unwanted, Unloved And Homeless

I am
an uneaten slice of bread
laying there going mouldy.

I am
a straying unwanted dog
abandoned by its owner.

I am
a lonely t-shirt
that no one wants to buy.

I am
an unloved animal
that they gave back to the pet shop.

I am
a dirty penny
that someone dropped in a drain.

I am
an unused scarf
that's hanging on an empty peg.

I am alone, unwanted and unloved.

Zoë Sheath (13)
Hethersett High School, Hethersett

Dreaming

Anyone can be anything,
and nothing can be everything.

You can have anything you choose,
from musical instruments to pairs of shoes.

You can be whatever you want to be,
from enormous elephant to a tiny flea.

All of this for an eyeshot away
what are you waiting for?
Rest your head and hit the hay.

Max Tarrant (13)
Hethersett High School, Hethersett

That Silly Little Thing!

Silly little thing, prancing around like he's king!
Gleaming eyes, devilish claws, it's a good thing animals don't have laws!
If animals had laws he would break them all,
Then he would be in prison next to the mall,
Where I would go shopping every day
To make sure he never sees me go away.
I would send him letters and write him cards
Even send presents from beneath the stars.
He would say, 'Thanks!' I would say, 'Bye!'
But he would say, 'No!' and then start to cry.
When he comes out I would be really glad
And when he scratches I would remind him
Of that time when he was bad.
But it got too much and he ran out of luck
And I said, 'See ya!' for the very last time.
I love him, I really do
I just wish I had the chance to tell him that.
Also that he was the best cat.
My silly little cat!

Lucy Sorrell (12)
Hethersett High School, Hethersett

I Am . . .

I am a prisoner
deranged and distraught.

I am a murderer
tormented by images.

I am Hell
evil and insane.

I am alone
lost and forgotten.

I am everything that is wrong in a person

I am black and not far from death!
I am . . . I am . . . I am . . .

Pearl Bodily (14)
Hethersett High School, Hethersett

And Love You I Will

I see you every day
Though I cannot mention your name
It feels like a stabbing pain
I know hearts that feel the same
Some people ask me
'So who's your secret love?'
I know I can't mention it
It's cooped up like a dove
I don't know how to tell you
I know I never will
You make me go crazy
Soon I'll be on the pill
I just wanted you to know that . . .
I loved you yesterday
And I love you still
I have always loved you
And love you I will.

Chloe Rix (12)
Hethersett High School, Hethersett

Moving!

Moving! When I was younger I moved and moved,
From place to place, one then another, never sure where I would end up.
Glad I stayed with my friends.
Same school!
Never changing!
A different adventure every time.
Scared! Excited!
Now finally! I'm still!
I've realised I don't like the adventure!
It scares me.
Moving! I hate it!
But the good things, I make new friends.
The bad things! I leave old friends.
Moving!
I hate it!

Jade Marie Fairall (13)
Hethersett High School, Hethersett

Phoebe

The way you wagged your tail before a walk.
You are my friend,
How I wished you could talk.
How your silky coat felt on my hand.
Now you lay there . . .
The way you look,
A frantic stare.
I wonder what's wrong.
I went to school,
But when I got home you were gone.
'She's sleeping,' says my mum.
I know what she means,
For I am not dumb.
Now it seems as if it's been rehearsed.
My third dog died, October the first.

Vikki Woodier (12)
Hethersett High School, Hethersett

I Am Me

Just because I'm not at the top
Doesn't mean you're better than me.
Just because I'm good at school
Doesn't make me a nerd.
Just because you don't know me
Doesn't mean you can judge me.
Just because I don't cause trouble
Doesn't mean I'm scared.
Just because I'm skinny
Doesn't mean I'm anorexic.
Just because I'm ugly
Doesn't mean I'm not beautiful inside.
Just because I'm not you
Doesn't mean I can't be me.
I am me, that's all I can be.

Zoe Reeve (13)
Hethersett High School, Hethersett

Football

Football, football, is so great
getting dressed is such a task
shinpads, socks, football boots
oh my lord that's such a task.
Then it's walking to the football pitch
warming up then running around
being put in teams and starting the match.

The match, that's a different thing, go in for a tackle
make a mistake and get a yellow card
it was only an accident but still it happens.
The match is over and you warm down and gather all the equipment
same old thing, when will we have a change?
We need some more action.
When will things change?

Lorraine Kutsirayi (13)
Hethersett High School, Hethersett

Stuff

Come home from school,
Bored out of my skin,
What to do? What to do?
What should I do?
Watch TV, nothing I like
Do some homework, yeah, sure, right.

It's Friday,
I'm happy about that,
Relaxing all weekend,
And that's a fact!
If it's cold,
I'll be snug as a bug in a rug!
If it's hot,
You won't see me a lot!

Caroline Chloe Lovick (13)
Hethersett High School, Hethersett

I Am . . .

I am the poison ivy that chokes the tree
I am the empty beer bottle in your dead child's hand.

The cancer cell, slowly killing you from the inside.
I am the eyes on the painting that follow you everywhere.

The wet cigarette in the side gutter.
The ruthless leader for a needy country.
I am the poisoned gas in the warm, thick air.
I am the one in the corner of the mirror, you know isn't there.

I am the dead flower, in the coloured garden.
I am the flight that was cancelled for no reason.
I am life!
I am society.
I am a lie.

Tim Lee (13)
Hethersett High School, Hethersett

Beanz

Mischievous, cunning, such as a jester, is my Westie
Take this ordeal, and you'll see
What it's like to live with Beanz
He was slouched in a comfortable pose
Sitting there, licking his nose
I cried in disgust, I told thee
He slumped; then jumped onto my knee
'Get off!' I shrugged, I asked him please
Jumping onto my face, he pleads
'No, no, no! That hurts!' I screamed
He barked, whined and he beamed
For he seemed to enjoy my face
Much to my disgrace
All this struggle, just in one day, living with Beanz.

Hayley McCarthy (12)
Hethersett High School, Hethersett

This Love Isn't Fake

I felt so closed up, but then I saw you.
And for once in a lifetime, I knew that this was true.
You make me feel free, and unafraid to just be me.
You're not like the others, you're funny, kind and sweet.
I can picture you and me, walking down the street.
People don't see you the way I do,
they say you're a chav, but they don't have a clue,
because they don't know you the way I do.
You're the only one who understands the real me.
You told me you love me, for who I am,
and adore my personality.
But loving you made me an outcast,
they think I love you as a joke.
But I don't care what they say, because you're my special bloke.

Gemma Stapleford (12)
Hethersett High School, Hethersett

Through The Dark

Wandering, wandering through the dark.
Nowhere to go, nowhere to stay.
Watching and waiting in the dark.
Looking above and only seeing grey.
Hoping that someone will save me from my pain.
There is no afterlife. Just the dark.
There is no life after death. Just the dark.
Nothing, nothing, fading away.
No one wants me so I can't stay.
Goodbye life, goodbye friends.
Remember me, remember me.
I shall always be
Wandering, wandering through the dark.

Kaylyn Calaz (13)
Hethersett High School, Hethersett

My Life

I don't believe in fairytales and other happy things
I never see them around
I think they've all been stolen and have been bound
By chains made from steel hate
But maybe that's their fate
Where's all the colour gone?
It's been replaced by black and white
Everyone is glum here
No one brave enough to fight
What I need is a hero
To save me from this place
To be my life and saviour
From now on my life is not a race.

Megan Annie Taylor (13)
Hethersett High School, Hethersett

Never Again

He was there, then gone
I stood there very still
Would I be alone forever?
This thought made me ill.

Never again would I see him
His eyes that glow in the dark
Now there was a hole in my heart
Surely it would make a mark.

I could feel the tears running down my face
It was so sad
It was like a part of me was missing
The feeling was driving me mad.

Falean Mussett (12)
Hethersett High School, Hethersett

Writing A Poem

It's harder than you think you know,
trying to think of the ideas to help me write it
but I have to do it,
if not I'll get in trouble,
so I guess I'll keep trying,
in fact, I think I've got an idea . . .

It's harder than you think you know,
trying to think of the ideas to help me write it
but I have to do it,
if not I will get in trouble,
so I guess I will keep trying,
in fact, I think I've got an idea . . .

Freddie Tarrant
Hethersett High School, Hethersett

Grandma

You and me together,
Through sun and stormy weather,
I thought you were forever,
But it doesn't seem.
We always had so much fun,
I knew you were the only one,
To help me through the hardest days,
It always seemed that way.
One day you were gone,
You said you would always be there,
But somehow I knew you were there,
Even though I couldn't see you.

Louisa Sutherland (12)
Hethersett High School, Hethersett

My Family

Sisters, sisters are so grumpy
Sisters, sisters are so horrible
Brothers, brothers always cry
Brothers, brothers always sleep
Mums, mums always get grumpy with you
Mums, mums always make you do your homework
Dads, dads never listen
Dads, dads never help
Nans, nans always on the phone
Nans, nans never get off the phone
Grandads, grandads always working
Grandads, grandads never stop working.

Alisha Haze (11)
Hethersett High School, Hethersett

Birthday Time!

Early morning, rise and shine, today's a special day,
Wake up Mum! Wake up Dad! Today's my birthday,
I open my cards, I open my presents, I wonder what I'll get?
A book! A bear! A gift voucher! And a very special net,
Run downstairs, what's for breakfast? My favourite, eggs and ham!
Now to put on my brand new dress, the one from Aunty Pam,
It's time to cut my birthday cake and blow the candles out,
I close my eyes and make a wish but I can't tell you what it's about,
It's time for a special dinner, chips then chocolate fondue,
I finish it all up and even have seconds too,
But it is now time for bed after a very exciting day,
So I lay my head on my pillow, and slowly drift away.

Alicia Camille Arnold (13)
Hethersett High School, Hethersett

Carly

My dog, Carly, was as sweet as anything.
Sadly she's dead and gone to her bed.

She was always under the table so we put her bed under the table.

The grave is in the garden
I pass by the grave
She was always a nice dog.

She always likes her walks in the wood
Especially in the winter, she loved the snow.

I will always love Carly and she knows her memory
I will always hold dear.

Kai Nudds (11)
Hethersett High School, Hethersett

Campfire

The flames flicker and dance in the cold winter night,
warming the hearts of those sitting around it.

The old and wise tell tales of past campfires,
to young and eager ears.

Joy, happiness but no tears.

The warm orange glow - a wonderful sight.

The atmosphere jolly and light.

Curling smoke joins laughter in the air,
These are the moments we want to cherish and share.

Joe Lincoln (12)
Hethersett High School, Hethersett

The Meaning Of Luke

L is for likeable, laughing, lucky and loopy.
U is for understanding.
K icking moves on a skateboard.
E njoying life to the full and enjoying being me.

Luke Heels (11)
Hethersett High School, Hethersett

Hallowe'en

Yet again it's Hallowe'en, a time to make small children scream.
I got on my costume and walked out the door.
To see my house covered in cream.
I went indoors and picked the mop off the floor.
I went outside and cleaned the house.
A child approached and said trick or treat.
I went to get the bowl of sweets but I tripped on my cat's toy mouse.
I got back to my feet,
and hit into my TV screen.
I've changed my mind
I hate Hallowe'en!

Ashley Mills (12)
Hethersett High School, Hethersett

Sunday Walk

We set off early on our Sunday walk.
Usually just Dad and I,
The only people we see are walking their dogs.
The sun is coming up, shining through clouds.
Beams of sunlight across the sugar beet field.
Down the path, by the wood.
The little stream is full because of the recent rain.
The trees make a tunnel over our heads.
Through trees today, we could see a hare and later, a cat.
If you're quiet you hear the birds, sometimes a woodpecker.
This is the best way to start a Sunday.

William Benstead (11)
Hethersett High School, Hethersett

My Grandad's Cancer

When I first heard I was in a shock
my mind couldn't think straight
The doctor said we found out a little too late.
My grandad's cancer has spread and spread,
all around and up in his head.
The doctor said there was a 9 in 10
chance he's got it and could die,
wow, from what I can remember time has flew by.
It's not a surprise from all the smoking you've done
I love you loads and loads,
and from now on I'm gonna take all the right roads.

Ellen Astbury-Dennis (12)
Hethersett High School, Hethersett

The Sea

The sea is like a lion,
Roaring away,
The sea is like mountains,
Reaching the sky,
The sea is like a washing machine,
Going back and forth, back and forth,
The sea is like a tsunami,
Rushing to the sand,
The sea is like a mob of people,
Running and charging.

Katie Utting (13)
Hethersett High School, Hethersett

I Am

I am a baby Labrador, joyful and energetic.
I am the inside of a coat, offering warmth to the human body.
I am a singer, entertaining those who care to listen.
I am mustard, fierce and fiery, spicy and enriching to plain meat.
I am a newspaper, imparting information to the world.
I am an unread book, waiting patiently to be opened.
I am a young child, who eagerly awaits Santa.
I am a cloud, drifting across a pale blue sky.
I am a comedy, delivering heart-warming laughter to the world.
I am Barack Obama, offering hope to the world.

Robert Stocks (13)
Hethersett High School, Hethersett

He Called

He called.
He said I could come.
Suddenly I was on the plane.
Excited, smiling, sleeping.
I saw him. I jumped. He fell.
Weeks later, crying, sad, sleeping.
Walking away, I saw the pain in his eyes.
I looked away.
Shouted, 'I love you,' as I walked away.
Pain inside.

Kayla Aughinbaugh (13)
Hethersett High School, Hethersett

Moving Home

The thought of moving house can be rather scary,
but then as my mum said it's normal to feel wary.
After all a house is your home,
somewhere to feel safe - not alone!
But 18 months on, my thoughts rarely wander
to the house where I was born, even though
at the time I had felt rather torn.
A new house feels like meeting a stranger.
Before you know it you realise there is no real danger
and your new house has become a home!

Heather Mackay (14)
Hethersett High School, Hethersett

Boys Before Friends?

Sorrow cloaks our friendship like the darkness at night
My boastful words slashes our alliance like a scalpel
If our glares could destroy we would be inanimate.

Despise clouds our eyes, but with sorrow included
We are fixed in a dilemma, a monstrous one at that.

How could she act so black-heartedly
I met him first, she just saw him
She fancies him, so what?
I don't care what she thinks, I'm going to ask him out.

Lucas Anthony (13)
Hethersett High School, Hethersett

The World Cup

The greatest prize of all and England are there
Will they win? Maybe not but still
England are there, England are there.
It would be good if we win so we could live 1966 all over again
England are there, England are there.
They have Rooney, Gerrard and Lampard to boost the team
So will the cup come back to England for the first time in 44 years
Or will we get pipped again?
England are there, England are there.

Scott Grimes (13)
Hethersett High School, Hethersett

In The Car

In the car, in the dark
Having a laugh, apparently going to a park.
Trees swaying, wind blowing,
Mind cold and me not knowing.
Not knowing where I was actually going.
We came to a sign, that wasn't much
My hands were leaning on the handle, clutched.
Suddenly, we were there, there we were.
Going to see Santa!

Laura Waterman (14)
Hethersett High School, Hethersett

My Animal Poem

Butterflies are so colourful that the sun reflects on the butterfly.
Their wings are tall, they shine like a star.
The patterns on their wings are colourful.
Their bodies are very fluffy that keeps them warm.

Their eyes are very small
And they are black eyes that looks like a ball.
Their feelers are very long,
They look like eyelashes.

Billy Howard (11)
Hethersett High School, Hethersett

Hallowe'en Night

Hallowe'en night!
The pumpkins are alight.
What can I wear to give people a fright?
A witch I could be, which is pale and white.
I have some spiders which might do the trick
And get on people's wick.
A broomstick would be handy to carry my candy
What a dandy night!

Georgia Gooch (14)
Hethersett High School, Hethersett

If Ever I Came Face To Face With A Shark

If ever I came face to face with a shark
I think I would die before it touches
Those death-eating eyes and that wide opening jaw
Which would surely kill you if it closes on you
They move as if they are playing Operation
Their quick bullet-like movement is hard to anticipate
As you look for an escape
Quick, get out of the water or *snap!*

Nathan Peck (13)
Hethersett High School, Hethersett

I Am . . .

I am a balloon ready to pop
I am a kettle ready to whistle
I am a light switch ready to be turned on
I am a firework ready to explode
I am a football ready to be kicked
I am a key ready to be turned
I am a ringing phone ready to be answered
I am a sweet ready to be eaten.

Sammy Jaber
Hethersett High School, Hethersett

I Am . . .

I am the reason everybody speaks.
I am the reason we all have sore feet.
I am the reason we all had a laugh.
I am the reason we all got a telegraph.
I am the reason we all had depression.
I am the reason we all got detention.
I am the reason we all got caught doing theft.
I should have thought about my actions at school before I left.

Jackson Tamaiparea (14)
Hethersett High School, Hethersett

I Am . . .

I go to school every day
Have homework every evening
Friends and family on the weekend
Seems like the only time there is to spend.

With a dad and mum
A sister and me
How hard can life be?

Hollie Hutchings (13)
Hethersett High School, Hethersett

My Present

It's new
It's blue
It's bright bolt of light
It's fast and smooth
It's Friday
It's my birthday
It's my bike.

Aaron Moralee (11)
Hethersett High School, Hethersett

Mondays (A Nonsense Poem)

It started off one Monday morning,
Suddenly I started yawning,
I really thought today would be boring
Then as I rolled out of bed
A little man said in my head,
'Good morning girl
How are we today?'
I started to panic, I was going mad
My brain went blank
I couldn't think
It was that afternoon
That changed the way I thought of a Monday
I woke up later in a white sheeted bed
It wasn't my own I thought in my head
Then I looked around,
Presents galore
Suddenly the little man popped into my head and said,
'Sorry about this awful day, I didn't realise
I would scare you in that way.'
Soon my body hurled to the ground
You can imagine what happened then
That all happened on a Monday morning
As soon as the day was dawning.

Rebecca Newman-Matthews (11)
Impington Village College, Impington

Love

The day I saw him
the first time my heart skipped a beat
and my eyes stared just at him.
I thought to myself, *he's the one, the only one for me.*
I looked into his brown sparkling eyes
just twinkling in the distance,
I can only see him, just him,
no one else, just him,
                    I love him, I do, I do.

Florence Hodgson-Kerry (11)
Impington Village College, Impington

Him

I love him.
The way his big brown eyes look into mine.
His warm hands touch mine.
His soft lips touch mine.
I love him.

When we're together I know it's right.
I feel special when I'm around him.
When he looks at me, it's right.
His brown soft fringe hanging over one eye.
When we're together I know it's right.

In the evening when we sit together,
looking over the beach.
The warm sun beaming on us.
The soft sand underneath us.
I am well and truly in love.
In the evening when we sit together,
looking over the beach.

I love him!

Olivia Brooklyn (12)
Impington Village College, Impington

Why?

Why are they walking away from me?
Why are they over there?
I thought they were my friends,
Friends forever,
Best mates for life,
Call it whatever you like,
Don't they like me
Or are they just playing a trick?
Why?

Megan Roberts (12)
Impington Village College, Impington

The Girl Across The Street

See that girl across the street,
The one I've been longing to meet.
She flashes a lovely smile,
Then stares at me for a while.
Then she says hi to me,
I blush and smile speechlessly.
Then she walks away from me,
I hope we meet again Cindy.
When she left I filled with glee,
And dreamt about her hugging me.
My heart beats rapidly just for her,
I can't resist her powerful lure.
I was a man, a man with pride,
But there's something about her I cannot hide.
Please tell me why, I cannot cry.
Over a beauty, a beauty like Cindy.
See that girl across the street, the one I no longer long to meet.

Michael Johnson (11)
Impington Village College, Impington

The Ultimate Change

The world is changing
Plants and all,
Everything big and everything small,
Buildings, children and life itself,
People with great fortune and people with great wealth,
Animals bigger, better and stronger,
Soon they won't be able to last a lot longer,
Buildings growing, growing far,
That's all because of the way we are,
The world is bad and beings are sad,
Change is slowly driving me mad,
The environment was good
And now it's worse than it ever should,
If we work together to make it right,
This world could soon change to be very bright.

Emma Williams (11)
Impington Village College, Impington

Winter

The chilly breeze was blowing
Around the snowy winter's garden
Snowflakes were falling
And floating in the misty sky
Snowmen were standing there like ice
When they walked past
They gave you a warm, loving smile
Children were playing in the snow
Having fantastic fun with snowballs
Then they would snuggle up by the warm fire
Relaxing and having hot chocolate, yum
Icicles were forming on the conker tree
Drip-drop, drip-drop
The ice-cold drips were ice drips
Soon the freezing cold days will come to an end
And summer will come.

Chloe Dyson
Impington Village College, Impington

Single Bullet

Waving goodbye to my family,
My mother shed a tear,
My father stood emotionless,
Their hearts full up with fear.
We set off in the trenches,
Our hearts a heavy load,
Enemies stood before me,
In my new abode.
The guns were getting loaded,
Ready for a fight,
He wasn't on our side,
So I had to do what's right.
Everybody in the world,
Has a final day,
A single bullet to my chest,
Took my life away.

Meghan Clark (14)
Impington Village College, Impington

That Boy

As my lover walked away
All I could think about is what I did wrong
My heart bled with sorrow
I needed him
I want him
I saw him in my head
His lovely brown eyes looking into mine
I knew we were meant to be
I love him.

As the sun rose
I could remember the first time we met
I hoped we would be together forever
Share our love and joy
Why did we break up?
I miss you, please come back.

Laura Robinson & Katie Dyson (11)
Impington Village College, Impington

Food

I like to eat food,
It tastes really good,
I hate Brussels sprouts,
They make me want to shout,
My favourite food is chicken and chips,
I like to eat it with lots of dips,
When I go to the café,
I always have a hot latte,
I always want to go out to eat,
But when we walk it hurts my feet,
When we buy food it costs lots of money,
Especially a giant jar of honey,
I like to eat food,
It tastes really good.

Om Menon (11)
Impington Village College, Impington

Coca-Cola In The Can

The Coca-Cola in the can fizzed and popped,
bubbles of fury bursting to the top.
When someone takes and shakes it about,
all the bubbles go around and around.
At the fair the Coca-Cola stall is about to open,
a humongous crowd appears from the back.
They had better hurry up and get their Coke,
because it's going to go flat!

Harry Joshua Pendred (11)
Impington Village College, Impington

Change

Hey, have you ever wondered why things change?
One minute you're happy the next you're sad,
then you're upset then you're glad,
you change your house, you change your friends
everything changes in the end
can we trust anything to stay the same?
Change will drive me insane
I start to feel like everything's in vain
now it is sunny but then it'll rain
change is very freaky and extremely sneaky

I wonder if crime will ever change
I wonder if it'll break a habit
maybe it'll take care of a cute rabbit
one minute you're alive, the next you're dead
because you didn't listen to what the shouting boy said

Hit by a car
you've gone too far
change can be anything, anything at all
even going from short to tall
but just don't be a fool
be clever, be smart, stick to things like art
don't get violent, don't start a fight, don't go and kill because
it is not a game, it is real.

Nathan Sackey (13)
Kemnal Technology College, Sidcup

What A Life

Driving round in my new convertible, roof down.
Showing it off up and around town.
Feeling like I should wear a crown.
What a life.

It's hectic driving on the A2.
Texts and calls from you know who.
Now I'm feeling stressed and slightly blue.
Hectic life.

At the petrol garage, for a coffee or tea.
Bargain price, at 20p.
In my car I'm happy and free.
Amazing life.

Back in my car, with a smile on my face.
With a need for speed, let's start a race.
You couldn't catch me, or keep the pace.
Exciting life.

Flashing lights in the rear view mirror.
I get the need, to drive quicker.
In the corner of my eye I see a flicker.
A scary life.

The flicker I see, a 4 by 4.
Crashes into my new car's door.
Flips me over, I'm on the floor.
A frightened life.

On the floor, all cold and lonely.
Crying now, I wonder if only.
I was somewhere warm, nice and homely.
A broken life.

My heart slows down, there's no more tears.
I haven't felt this cold in years.
I suppose it's time to face my fears.
End of my life.

Josh Cook (16)
Kemnal Technology College, Sidcup

Run!

When you run a marathon
No you don't have to be an icon
You just have to be fit, get ready
You have to train hard, get steady.

Then the gun goes off
You run off hard but don't be a showoff!
You go off at a steady pace
But you realise you're running a race.

'Go on, keep going'
And you're one mile in
But you are slowing
So you've got to speed up if you're going to win.

Halfway through you 'hit the wall'
And you think you're going to stop
But you're only 50th over all
So you carry on if you want to get up top.

Then you find your second wind
And you feel just great
And you remember how the crowd grinned
But now you must meet your fate.

Finally with one mile to go
You think you're going to die
You've been running three hours so
To the end you must fly.

The race is over now
And you know what you have achieved
You finished in three ten, how?
Just because you believed.

Thomas Desborough (13)
Kemnal Technology College, Sidcup

My Life

In my life there's
so much confusion
I'm thinking hard to
find the solution
one minute it's
happiness and peace
next minute fire blowing
on the streets, the kids
in my school, think
they're so hard, bullying
kids and making followers
laugh,
if you look a
certain way the bullies
will make you never forget
they diss you hard until
you tick, they did it to me
but I stood
strong - strong and
tall, otherwise you'll
get picked
on and feel small
that's why I tone
up and feel
strong, so any man
comes to me
I'll always be
ready to fight
the fight and
be definitely steady.

Tashan Collins-McIntosh (14)
Kemnal Technology College, Sidcup

Perfect Plastic

Why do you compare yourself to the perfect pictures of me in magazines?
I may appear to be beautiful,
But all is not as it seems.
What you see is a cocoon of stiff silicone,
To shield me from Man's sharp sceptical view.

Why do you watch my music videos and wish you were me?
Paranoia possesses me at the sound of whispers,
My mind is riddled with threads of insecurities,
Am I not just like you?

The fame, fortune and fancy things,
I have it all but yet I still have a severed self-esteem.
I wish I could blend in with you all,
Not to have fake features,
And like a peacock; have natural beauty.

Don't ever wish you were me.

This life is not what it is cracked up to be,
I live with the silent humiliation of faking splendour,
And being a small pawn in this huge facade we call the 'industry'.

I wish I were you,
Flaws and all.
No artificial perfection,
But an air of imperfect beauty,
That radiates from within.

You are beautiful as you are,
Without the perfect plastic,
And the modern surgery.

Warren Wellington (15)
Kemnal Technology College, Sidcup

Homeless Man

I am a homeless man
Free roaming the street,
I have dirty clothes
And stinky feet.

I often shoplift
And ride in trolleys,
But wait if it's raining
I'll need someone's brolly.

When I get drunk
I'm very scary,
So watch out you
And don't get lairy.

My name is Jim,
I think?
Oi! You
Go buy me a drink.

Lots of people come and go
Especially teens on their bikes,
When they ride by I say
'Oi! You wanna fight?'

When I go to bed at night
Curl up on the street floor,
Tomorrow's a new day
People harass me no more.

David Dixon (12)
Kemnal Technology College, Sidcup

Photo Day

Today is photo day at school,
I've got to look nice and cool,
But then you have to have one,
Who always thinks they look the best.

When I get to school I'm going to look my best,
I'm not going to look like I'm in a vest,
But then again there is that one,
Who always thinks they look the best.

I'm in the photo shoot now,
I'm scared that I am going to look like a cow,
And guess who is in front of me?
The one who thinks they look the best!

She is in the photo shoot now and looks great,
This is making me feel like I want to wait,
The photographer said she looked so good.

Now I am angry and I could go mad,
I go in all scraggy and tired,
I feel like I have expired,
As he took my picture I pulled a moody face,
I'll take the photo home thinking what my mum will say?

When I get home she is going to want to look,
Maybe I'll hide it in my boot,
'Come on then, let me see'
I held out the picture and her face suddenly dropped!

Harry Stapley (12)
Kemnal Technology College, Sidcup

Me In A Corner

Me in a corner
Sad and alone
Mum and Dad shouting, overpowering my thoughts
There is a fire of fear in my belly
Things smashing over walls
I feel sick from all the hatred and sadness

The fire is growing and growing
Till I break out in to tears
Mum and Dad still at it
I feel weak and helpless
I want it to stop
I want my old mum and dad back

No one can save me
I am in a ball
Hands round my legs scared and distraught
Trying to think of a happy place
But just can't
I need someone to hold on to

I stand up with courage
Walk to them and say
'Stop, stop it, please.'
I run back to my corner,
The noise stopped
It is broken again by a 'Sorry.'

Jay Smith (12)
Kemnal Technology College, Sidcup

The Last Second . . .

Many children meet the end,
Their parents make them lie,
Different children greet the trend,
As every second passes by . . .

All I feel is pain,
As these children die,
Many children join the chain,
As every second passes by . . .

When little babies groan,
They're greeted with a smack,
Again they shout and moan,
As they wish the clock turns back . . .

They're beaten too and throw
But the abuse just gets worse,
They hope the pain would go,
But the parents start to curse.

PS
Child abuse is not a game
It is a force to be reckoned
Beaten till made lame,
As they meet their last second . . .

Jae Siley-Watt (12)
Kemnal Technology College, Sidcup

Climate Change

Climate change takes lives
children, husbands and wives
could you imagine a life?
with no children, a husband or a wife?
It would be lonely with no friends
no work and no money to spend
roads to rivers
rivers to seas
houses demolished
nowhere to sleep
no crops for the people in need
there goes our daily feed!
Our planet is not being treated right
but it won't go without a fight
if we start to act now, our Earth will be happy
here is some ways how:
try to walk instead of the car
if you are going to the local shops
or at the farm collecting crops
all it takes is a little walk
others do it so why can't you?

Max Turner Howard (12)
Kemnal Technology College, Sidcup

Liar, Liar

How it takes you like a UFO,
Making you lie more, more and more.
Every day you have a new excuse,
How the chain becomes more loose.

How you join every gang on the street,
Making you 'most wanted' on the police's sheet.
Maybe even one day you will kill and run,
And be chased by police with laser guns.

Your hatred will become darker each day,
Making you lie and kill on your violent way.
You won't care about others in this state of evilness,
And in your path of destruction you will leave a mess.

But of course, as all criminals do,
You will be arrested by police task force 2.
You will be taken to a judge to consider your fate,
'It's a life sentence, Mr Zate!'

You are locked in a cell, cold as the ice,
And your only company are rats and mice.
Liar, liar!

Gabrial Arusoae (13)
Kemnal Technology College, Sidcup

The Last Breath

The warm air he breathes out
We didn't even get to see the young Brussels sprout
But that's life isn't it?

A youth to another youth stabbing every day
Life's a struggle, you work to get paid
But that's life isn't it?

He falls to the ground, never to stand up
Makes you cry, you never get to say your goodbye
But that's life isn't it?

They say that life is short
But is it supposed to be that short?
A youth getting caught,
In the right place at the wrong time?
Or
In the wrong place at the right time?
Maybe I'm just saying stuff to make a rhyme . . .
But while you're taking time to read my poem
Another youth has taken their last breath . . .

Adefisayo Adeshina (12)
Kemnal Technology College, Sidcup

The Game

A new game is out, it has to be mine
Have to get to the store, gotta be on time
A crowd rushes in, I'm in there too
The noise is so loud it sounds like a zoo.

I've got to go, gotta get my game
Wait . . . oh no I forgot the name!
I've found it! Gotta get in line
Soon I have to go home, almost out of time

I'm at home, about to play my game
'Time for bed.'
Noooo! So close. That's so lame!

Miles Taylor (12)
Kemnal Technology College, Sidcup

Mum And Dad

You can make decisions but not for me
You can be right
I'm not too dumb to fight for what I want myself
I know what's best for me
I know it all
Mum and Dad just hit the wall

I can choose my life
I choose who I want to be
That's how you made me

Mum and Dad
I want you to let me grow up
Let me be free!

Mum and Dad say I'm right
Mum and Dad show me the best
Mum and Dad save my life

Mum and Dad, I will show you.

Pelham Botley (13)
Kemnal Technology College, Sidcup

Dear God

Dear God if You're truly there
Listen to me as I say this prayer.
Many are dead and many are gone
Are they victims of fate, or is it the Devil's work been taken on.

Or is it the way that the cookie crumbles?
Or just the way that you make them humble?
You've given free will but they've taken it for granted
You said don't forget to finish what you've started.

You recognise that there's good and bad in the world
And the differences between Heaven and Hell.
Some try to cheat death, others just except it
And there's good and bad; why can't the bad be corrected?

You say everybody's equal yet there was a slave trade,
With people getting sold for a daily wage.
Slavery has been abolished but we're still on the same page
And maybe that's why some people feel the rage!

Lewis Kupperblatt (15)
Kemnal Technology College, Sidcup

My Football Poem

Football is more than a game,
It's a deep routed passion.
I feel for football,
As girls feel for fashion.

When I have that first touch,
It feels as though I'm the only person alive.
Like you feel,
When you're with your wives.

And when I score,
I feel like I've accomplished something,
Almost excited,
Like when you're a kid.

But the best part of all,
Is not knowing what will happen next.

Matthew Brennan (13)
Kemnal Technology College, Sidcup

The True Feelings

I get these times
When I would never hear chimes
So when I feel like hiding
I'll sit at the back all sad
I'd shut my eyes and think happy,
But sometimes it's hard,
'Cause all I would think is
Are people looking at me,
Do I fit in?
And the answer would be no
I'd think to myself
If I was a Sikh
It would be different
Because they believe everyone's equal
One day my life would change
Things would be different
I'll sit waiting till that day.

Martina Marshall (12)
Pakefield Middle School, Pakefield

Jesus

You need Jesus, to help you through
Your life may be hard
But there is hope yet.

There is a hole in you
Waiting to be filled
A God-like hole
Crying out for love.

You need Jesus,
To help you through
Steer away from this life
Choose Heaven not Hell.

There is a cry in your heart
Desiring love and compassion
Jesus is on offer
100% *free!*

You need Jesus
To help you through
You desire love
Someone to understand.

So find out more
Go on, google salvation
Check out Jesus.com
He's free; He's for you.

You need Jesus
To help you through.

Thomas Pointon (11)
Pakefield Middle School, Pakefield

Greed Is War

Wanting more than your fair share,
Is my definition of greed
When one person starts
The rest will pay
This will lead to war.

Money, power, land
Death, poverty, homelessness
They all lead to war
Who wants to kill?
Who wants to hurt?

It makes me sad
To think of this
This issue I fear
Is getting too big
World War Three seems imminent.

Is it too late
To stop this crime
Or is there something we can do?

Give back the money
Share all the power
Let go of the land
Don't take revenge
Try helping the poor.

Learn to forgive
Then World War Three looks more dim.

Robert Sharp (12)
Pakefield Middle School, Pakefield

Praise The Person Who Made It All

On a Sunday morning,
I get out of bed.
I get ready for church,
and think in my head.

I think of the things,
I will say to the Lord.
Things that are good,
and things that are hard.

On the way in the car,
I see trees and flowers.
Sometimes it is sunny,
sometimes there are showers.

I watch the birds,
and all the creatures.
On the way in the car,
I see the amazing features.

As we go through puddles,
we splash through mud.
We go over speed bumps too fast,
and land with a thud.

I thank our God,
as we arrive at the hall.
All the things I have seen,
I praise him who made it all.

Nicole Weatherley (12)
Pakefield Middle School, Pakefield

I'm Happy

I'm happy when I play out
I'm happy when I'm on my laptop
I'm happy when I do things
I'm happy when I'm with my friends
I'm happy when I'm on rides
I'm happy when I'm happy.

Lucy Rudd (11)
Pakefield Middle School, Pakefield

War!

We was alright once,
We're not any more
There was a fight that wasn't alright
It was all about power you see,
Now that fight is a war.

Everything shattered,
Everything clattered
Families crusted
They tried to rush
They couldn't get out in time!

We was alright once
We're not any more
There was a fight that wasn't alright
It was all about power you see,
Now that fight is a war.

There are evacuees everywhere,
On the trains, in the country,
All going to fight
All cowering in fright.

We was alright once,
We're not any more
There was a fight that wasn't alright,
It was all about power you see,
Now that fight is a war.

Daniel Jackson (11)
Pakefield Middle School, Pakefield

Ryan Is Ryan

Just because I am clever does not mean I am a nerd
Just because I like reading does not mean I read a lot
Just because I like cooking does not mean I am a girl
Just because I am weak does not mean you can bully me
Just because I play games a lot
does not mean I am a computer geek.

Ryan Sharp
Pakefield Middle School, Pakefield

War!

Thousands go out
Hundreds come back!
Think they can win -
Think again!
No one knows what will happen.
If you survive you're lucky
If you don't well . . .
All I have to say is
Think!
Watch their eyes as you see them go
See the fear, dragging feet so very slow.

Duty first, lives to be lost
Must win the war at any cost.

Grandfather was a pilot in World War II
Lost his life in the sky so blue
Wouldn't want to die again
Haven't they learnt their lesson.

Thousands go out
Hundreds come back!
Think they can win -
Think again!
No one knows what will happen
If you survive you're lucky
If you don't well . . .

Scott Dunning (11)
Pakefield Middle School, Pakefield

I'm Me!

Because I try hard in lessons doesn't mean I'm a teacher's pet
Because I like sports doesn't mean I'm a freak
Because I'm quiet doesn't mean I can't stand up for myself
Because I don't get into trouble doesn't mean I'm not cool
Because I don't fight anyone doesn't mean I can't
I am who I am no one can change me
Like it or *not*.

Hannah Crebbin (11)
Pakefield Middle School, Pakefield

What's The Point?

I've been bullied before
So what's the point?
I'm small but that doesn't make me different
So what's the point?
Pushing and shoving and being downright rude,
So what's the point?
You say I'm ugly, have you seen yourself lately
So what's the point?
You say I'm fat, do I really look it?
So what's the point?
I've changed school, so I don't want it to start again
So what's the point?
Because I have more friends than you
It doesn't make me a loser
So what's the point?
You say I'm not perfect but who is?
So what's the point?
Just because I'm shy doesn't mean I can't stand up for myself.

I will carry on being myself,
People need to accept me for who I am not what people believe.
And if you don't like me,
Just leave me alone!

What's the point in bullying?

Georgia Blane (12)
Pakefield Middle School, Pakefield

Friends And Families

Friends and families they mean a lot
We have them but some people have not
Friends are there for you whenever you're sad
Families are there for you that love you like mad.

Friends are people that you can trust
Your friendship is good so don't let it go bust
Families are there for you whenever you're bullied
By boys and girls in big black hoodies.

Rebecca Williams (12)
Pakefield Middle School, Pakefield

I Am Who I Am

Every day I think to myself
Wouldn't it be lovely to be a boy of wealth
But I am who I am
And I can't be changed

Some people say I am a teacher's pet
Because I am good in my lessons
But I am who I am
And I can't be changed

Sometimes I get called a girl
Because I hang around with them
But I am who I am
And I can't be changed.

I have been bullied for being shy
I guess I'm not that type of guy
Because I am who I am
And I can't be changed

A lot of people don't like me
And I don't know why
But all I can say is
I am who I am
And I can't be changed.

Kyle Bessey (12)
Pakefield Middle School, Pakefield

The Cod

The cod is a beautiful fish
But it is slowly disappearing from our seas.
Let me tell you how it happens
The cod is swimming in the sea
It gets dragged into the nets
Then it gets hauled on deck
They clip its gills so it can't breathe
Then it is hanged by its neck
Imagine all that just for you to eat.

Jacob Ayers (11)
Pakefield Middle School, Pakefield

Can't It Just Be

Bang! goes the gun, whack goes the fist
Why do some people have to be like this?
I'm wishing upon a shining star
Hoping that it will go very far
Can't there be a rainbow just over the sea
Instead of crime and killing, can't it just be.

Children weeping all alone
But why are they on their own
I see some homeless when I walk along the street
And I feel sad about the people I meet.
Can't there be a rainbow just over the sea
Instead of poor and poverty, can't it just be.

Alcohol and drugs, where does it end
I can see death just around the bend
Crashing cars, flashing lights
These things happen day and night
Can't there be a rainbow just over the sea
Instead of drugs and alcohol, can't it just be?

I wish upon a star each day and each night
Wishing these things will disappear out of sight.

Emily Lau (13)
Pakefield Middle School, Pakefield

The Poem About Billy Ace

Yes I'm small, but I'm still cool
Yes I'm cold hearted, but I'm still emotional
Yes I'm fat, but I'm still fast
Yes I'm in love, but I'm still on the boy's side
Yes I'm a learner, but it's only in class
Yes I'm getting told off, but it's for my friends
Yes I'm disabled, but I'm still me
Yes I'm being bullied, but I'm still hard
Yes I'm on drugs, but I'll never change
Yes I have found new mates, but you're first always
Yes I'm Billy, but I will still be the man.

Jesse Lee Wright (12)
Pakefield Middle School, Pakefield

Change!

My cat is called Milky and
she is very silky
but she can't be changed
My brother is called Bob and
he is such a snob
but he can't be changed
My dog is dark and
he likes to bark
but he can't be changed
My dad can get very mad
but he can't be changed
My sister can get lots of blisters
but she can't be changed
My mum can be very glum
but she can't be changed
My fish live in a dish
but they can't be changed
There are lots of people in this world
each one different
so don't call them names
it's not their fault, they can't be changed.

Ewan Sibbons (11)
Pakefield Middle School, Pakefield

War

War is a terrible thing
Guns firing bombs dropping
Knives shining in the sun

Men and women go to war
Leaving their families behind
Lots go, some come back

These unfortunate men that have died
Their wives are at home
All they have of him is a photo or a memory
Dreaming about him at his grave.

Callum Howe (11)
Pakefield Middle School, Pakefield

Prison

I wake up
I get dressed
I get ready
I go to school,

It's the same stuff day in, day out,

Do ya homework
Do ya chores
Do this then do that,

My brain is outta whack,

I'm over heatin'
Batteries depletin'
Feelin' run down
Gunned down,

I'm fed up with this repeated cycle every day
I want it to go away,

I'm an animal caged in a prison,
Now I'm breaking out.

Konna Ashmore
Pakefield Middle School, Pakefield

I Always Tell The Teacher

I always tell the teacher, that just because I slouch,
it doesn't mean I'm not listening.

I always tell the teacher, that just because I watch TV,
it doesn't mean I won't learn.

I always tell the teacher, that just because I don't look at her
when she is speaking,
it doesn't mean I don't work well in groups.

I always tell the teacher, that just because I don't write neatly enough,
it doesn't mean I'm not going to get good grades.

I always tell the teacher, that just because I don't concentrate enough,
it doesn't mean I won't make my ambition.

Elliot Bagge (12)
Pakefield Middle School, Pakefield

School Life

I like school don't get me wrong
Although some days seem so long
So what if maths is lame
I try to think of it as a game
Add this, take that, how many
Multiples of three
But all I can think about is
What's for tea?
DT is my thing
My fairground ride and my keyring
'Fantastic effort,' said Mr Jordan
This certainly isn't a lesson
I get bored in
ICT is also great
The best bits being powerpoint,
Excel, I can create
I suppose school is not that bad
But at 3.20, when that bell rings
I am so glad.

Rhys Brown (11)
Pakefield Middle School, Pakefield

My Life!

My name is Eliot and I am as happy as a hippy
I like to listen to music which is dip, dop, dippy
I like DT and a little bit of art
I don't eat beans because they make me . . .
I like to play on my PS3
I am an expert on Call Of Duty.
I am friendly and also quite kind
I also have an extremely intelligent mind
Until it comes to history
Where everything seems to be a mystery
I also have a very good appetite
Chocolate, crisps and my favourite . . . cheese
And I don't know anyone who disagrees.

Eliot Bird (11)
Pakefield Middle School, Pakefield

Why Do It?

Why is there much bullying?
Why do people do it?
Why do people think it's ok?
Why do people say it?
Why do people think it makes them cool?
Because it doesn't
There's too much hate.

Why do people do it?
Why do people put up with it?
Why do people have so much anger to do it?
Why do people go to school to put up with it?
There's too much hate.

Why do people thump and say horrible things?
Why do people run away?
Why don't people tell someone
or stand up to them?
because running away doesn't help
and you can only be who you are and that's how you are.

Freya Mickleburgh (11)
Pakefield Middle School, Pakefield

This Is Me

My name is Chantelle
I love lots of things like singing and dancing
and happy things.
I like cookies and cakes as well as pop music,
I like English and art but not DT
History is bad but not geography.

I'm a caring person
as everyone knows
with tons of friends
and pets as you know.
I only dislike a few things
like sour food
and other things.

Chantelle Dewbery (11)
Pakefield Middle School, Pakefield

Soldier's Heart

Legs running,
Breath rasping,
Heart beating.

Guns blazing,
Rockets firing,
Knives flashing.

Friends dying,
Brothers slaughtered,
Family murdered.

Legs running,
Breath rasping,
Heart frozen.

Each year,
Thousands leave,
Hundreds return . . .

The terrible call of war.

Ellis Langley (12)
Pakefield Middle School, Pakefield

Doesn't Make Me

Just because I don't hang with the cool people,
doesn't make me a loser.
Just because I'm not pretty,
doesn't make me hideous.
Just because I don't smoke,
doesn't make me lame.
Just because I listen in lessons,
doesn't make me a nerd.
Just because I have nice things,
doesn't make me spoilt.
Just because I'm not skinny,
doesn't make me obese.
Maybe you think these things are true,
but I'm sure people think them about you.

Chelsea Smith (12)
Pakefield Middle School, Pakefield

Change

Change is good some people say,
And everyone is changing day by day,
I'm changing I know I am,
They don't like change, they think it's a sham.
Lying, backstabbing, they don't care,
Oh my god, it's not fair,
They all left in the end!
Losing all of my self-esteem,
It's coming back so it may seem,
I've got some great mates,
But still some people hate.
I look at all those bullying boys,
I have to work with them oh joy, oh joy!
Some of them I like a lot
Some of them . . . or not.
People change and so do I,
I don't care what people think,
This is me, like it or lump it!

Katie Lambert (12)
Pakefield Middle School, Pakefield

Everywhere You Go

Everywhere you go
People on the streets
Hanging about on corners
Waiting for someone

No one they ever meet
Someone random
They get a thrill
From taking your life away

The police knock on your door
To tell the news
The person gets a sentence
Of about six years

But nothing compares to the sentence you face!

Charlotte Pell (12)
Pakefield Middle School, Pakefield

Untitled

Smoke, smoke, smoke
please don't smoke
it's bad for you, it can harm you, even kill you
just don't do it.

You can end up with different kinds of things
cancer
die young
kidney failure
Don't do it!

Smoke, smoke, smoke . . .
Don't smoke
Smoke, smoke, smoke . . .
you can feel the killing
Smoke moving around you
Smoke, smoke, smoke . . .
Just don't risk your life
Please!

Chelsie Wilson (12)
Pakefield Middle School, Pakefield

Accept Me For Who I Am

Accept me for who I am,
I am not nasty, I am nice
Accept me for who I am,
I am not big, I am small
Accept me for who I am,
I am not scary Mary,
I am a sweet little girl
Accept me for who I am,
I am not a fighter, I am brighter
Accept me for who I am,
I am not any trouble, doesn't make me a loser

So accept me for who I am
and always be nice to me
so accept me for who I am.

Charlotte Ann Girling (12)
Pakefield Middle School, Pakefield

The Three Girls

Arriving at school,
Going into the cold classroom,
Knowing they will be there,
The three girls . . .

Calling you names along the way,
Blah blah blah, ignoring it is no good,
It still hurts your feelings,
The three girls . . .

They wait there at your locker,
Waiting to do something else to you,
Scared wondering if you should go there,
The three girls . . .

At the end of the day,
They have finally gone,
You walk home knowing it will happen again tomorrow,
The three girls . . .

Emily Smith (11)
Pakefield Middle School, Pakefield

Best Friends

I have best friends
they are the people
the people that I can count on
they never let me down
and are always there for me
when I need them and
when they need me.
I am always there for them
and we all support each other
and when one of us is
feeling down
we see and talk about what it is about
and we try to solve the problem
by talking about it
and if we kept it inside we wouldn't be best friends.

Alysha Holmes-Thrower (12)
Pakefield Middle School, Pakefield

I Am Who I Am

Just because I don't hang around with you doesn't make you cooler,
Just because I am ugly doesn't make you pretty,
Just because I have big feet it doesn't make yours smaller,
I am who I am and you will never change me!

Just because my family is fat it doesn't make yours thinner,
Just because I can't dance it doesn't make you the best dancer in the world,
Just because I am tall it doesn't make you shorter,
I am who I am and you will never change me!

Just because I am smart doesn't make you any dumber,
Just because I don't have an iPhone doesn't make your phone any cooler,
Just because I love my mum doesn't make me a mummy's girl,
I am who I am and you can never change me!

Just because you are popular doesn't make me less popular
Just because I never fight doesn't make you any tougher,
Just because I am *different* doesn't mean you and me can't be friends,
I am who I am and you can never change me!

Lauren Bryant (11)
Pakefield Middle School, Pakefield

School

School is all right,
But the teachers make you write,
Once it's the end of school,
The teachers are in the hall,
People think my bike is rubbish,
I don't care if it smells like fish,
I like PE,
I dislike RE,
I play basketball,
People think it's lame,
But it's my game,
I like football,
Because I like running around with my mates,
Once I've left the school gates,
I'm ready to relax.

Jack Shuttleworth (11)
Pakefield Middle School, Pakefield

Forgive And Forget

Calling names
pushing and shoving
playing games
am I worth loving?

Titch and tiny
ugly and ratty
moany and whiny
I'm not that tatty.

Big and fat
stinky and smelly
they treat me like a rat
and laugh at my belly!

It's time to change
time to move on
time to forgive
and time to forget!

Lauren Hurren (12)
Pakefield Middle School, Pakefield

Leave Me Alone

Screaming and shouting out so loud
thinking you're cool acting so proud
who are you to control me
I have my own life can't you see
standing in the dark all on my own
looking at the ball you have just thrown
can't you just leave me alone.
Talking and stalking me all the time
whilst you are out committing crime
who's the better person, me or you?
It takes a long time when you're thinking things through
but you don't understand
because you're definitely banned
from my life like a cold stone
can't you just leave me alone.

Jatinder Bains (12)
Pakefield Middle School, Pakefield

Hypocrites

'These kids!' they say,
It happens every day,
They blame video games,
Movies, violence and cocaine,
'*Ban them!*' they scream,
But they are just being mean,
Who is it who makes video games?
Who directs the movies?
Who fights in wars?
Adults!
They think we are to fault,
But they don't know what I know,
They have hit an all time low,
Now they have reached the limit
Now they deserve the title . . .
Hypocrite!

George Litchfield
Pakefield Middle School, Pakefield

I Am Not

I am not a nerd
because I try,
I am not a teacher's pet
because they like me,
I am not a loser,
because I am not a rebel,
I am not boring,
because I don't mess around,
just because I have self-esteem
doesn't mean people can bring me down
I am not a baby or a wimp
because I don't jump off stuff,
just because I might have a future,
doesn't mean people can mess with it,
I am never 'really' happy,
even if I don't show it.

Jade Parker (11)
Pakefield Middle School, Pakefield

Guns Are No Fun!

Everybody's done it,
I mean who hasn't lied,
But is it right to do it,
After someone's died?

Why do they do it, for money, respect or fun?
Their whole life could be ruined, with the trigger of a gun.

It's a dark and eternal road,
Never to be walked,
And if you ever enter it,
Forever you'll be stalked.

Even if you don't get caught,
The memories will always haunt you,
The effects it has on the people around you,
Are devastating too.

Marcus Rhys Dyer (11)
Pakefield Middle School, Pakefield

Dog Beater

He kicks him about
And pulls his snout
He doesn't care if he hurts him
He throws him out without a doubt
He's a dog beater!
He drags him out into the garden
And leaves him out for hours
He's a dog beater!
I want to kick him out
And pull him about
I don't care if I hurt him
He's a dog beater
I want to drag him out
And leave him out for hours
He's a dog beater and he needs to change.

Savannah James (11)
Pakefield Middle School, Pakefield

My Aim

I walk to school there and back
how boring is that!
I can't wait to get to school
cause maths and English rule.

My hobbies are to sing and football too
but dancing is my goal, to be on stage
every day performing to the world.

My friends are important, my teachers are too.
To be successful in my career is all I want to do.
I have to focus, I know just what to do
English, maths and science will lead me through
I'll do my best to concentrate on what my teachers say
but I have to be honest
I will *be dancing one day!*

Katie Bibby (12)
Pakefield Middle School, Pakefield

Happy

I feel happy when I am with my friends.
I feel happy when it is my birthday.
I feel happy when it is Easter.
I feel happy when it is Christmas.
I feel happy when I am playing sports.
I feel happy when I am at the park.
I feel happy when I am on holiday.
I feel happy when I am with my cousins.
I feel happy when I play basketball with my dad.
I feel happy when I score a goal.
I feel happy when I read a book.
I feel happy when I eat something delicious.
I feel happy when I beat someone at a game.
I feel happy when I complete a game.

Jonathan He (13)
Pakefield Middle School, Pakefield

Happy Stuff

I feel happy
I go to school and feel happy
I like school
I get to school at 8.25 by walking
I like all lessons
I finish school at 3.20 by walking
My best friend is Emily Smith
I like my best friend
My nickname is: Lozza-Jade
But my real name is Lauren-Jade Bellward
I like all types of things
I like Me To You teddies
I like playboy
And I like parties and balloons.

Lauren-Jade Bellward (11)
Pakefield Middle School, Pakefield

Why?

Why is the world filled with such hate?
Murders and meanness, why?
It doesn't make people greater or have more mates,
It just fills everyone with anger and guilt.

Why is the world filled with such bullies?
Name calling and hurting people, why?
Some people think it's so cool, please,
It just makes people unhappy and sad.

Why is the world filled with so much boastfulness?
People trying to show they're better, why?
Saying you're better than others doesn't make you the best,
It just makes people feel unwanted.
Why?

Kim Harvey (11)
Pakefield Middle School, Pakefield

Troubled Lives

Some people enter the land of trouble,
knowing they will never return,
their parents try to stop them,
but they will never learn.

They take the drugs, and eat the bugs,
but never really care
and you'll never find them anywhere
with a cuddly teddy bear.

They grow into gangsters
beating up pranksters
and selling drugs all day
going up to grannies and asking for some money
and getting them to give their pay.

Sam Lockwood (11)
Pakefield Middle School, Pakefield

In Your Point Of View

I am intelligent, but not in your point of view
I have friends, but not in your point of view
My mum loves me, but not in your point of view
I have a house, but not in your point of view
I have people who care, but not in your point of view
I love my life, but not in your point of view
Your words still hurt me after all I have tried.

It's not just me
It's everyone else
You pick on them
Like you pick on me.

Stop hurting me inside and out
because some day soon you will have your doubts.

Josh Blowers (12)
Pakefield Middle School, Pakefield

Same Place, Same Time

She stands there waiting for me,
Just after 3rd period, *same place, same time*
I stand there waiting for *it*, to happen,
Waiting for her to pull my hair and rip my homework everywhere.
When I get home I don't get noticed
My parents just lay there watching TV
Drinking and smoking
I just go upstairs to wipe my cheeks
From the tears of mascara
I look at what a state I look
Then I lay on my bed silently until 10pm
Then I go to sleep waiting for the next 3rd period
Same place, same time!

Charley-Anne Newrick (12)
Pakefield Middle School, Pakefield

Milly

My dog's name is Milly,
she is small and cute,
sometimes she is very silly,
her best friend is Bracken,
her enemy is Alfie,
and she's always having a wee.
She has dangly ears,
and puppy-dog eyes.
Milly and Bracken run around like deers,
but sometimes she gives me a little sigh.
She is very cute
unlike a boot
and she's my dog.

George Edwards (12)
Pakefield Middle School, Pakefield

Why, Oh Why, Oh Why

Why, oh why did you decide to do it?
Why, oh why did you choose me?
Why, oh why did you make me feel like a bottomless pit?
Why, oh why, oh why.

Why, oh why do you say I'm really lean?
Why, oh why are you so nasty?
Why, oh why are you so mean?
Why, oh why, oh why.

Why, oh why do you make me feel bad?
Why, oh why do you call me names?
Why, oh why because it makes me feel sad,
Why, oh why, oh why.

Jordan Taylor (12)
Pakefield Middle School, Pakefield

Boundaries

Whenever I come out of my front door
My mother's voice echoes down to me
'Remember this, take care with that,'
It's all because it's not as safe
Not as safe as it used to be.

Now I understand the forever-long rants that drive me
Senseless with boredom
All about how safe it was
How safe it used to be.

Now I'm in the back of a car, a stranger's car!
All because I didn't listen, I didn't listen to how it's not as safe
Not as safe as it used to be.

Jack Hales (11)
Pakefield Middle School, Pakefield

What Is The World Doing?

Drugs, drugs, drugs
Alcohol, alcohol, alcohol
Crime, crime, crime
What is the world doing?

Youngsters acting cool, smoking, doing drugs
Adults getting trashed
Murderers killing innocent people
What is the world doing?

Let's ban drugs coming into this country
Make sure people have two or three beers
Murderers should be locked up forever
Let's help change this world.

Daniel Lark (13)
Pakefield Middle School, Pakefield

Me!

My name is Yasmin
I love to prance around
singing and dancing
is all around.

I love my music
as well as my food
I love cookies and milk
and I love you too.

I'm a loving person
as you can guess
I'll care for you
and as much as you wish.

Yasmin Levett (11)
Pakefield Middle School, Pakefield

Save The Environment

Save the environment, use solar power to get electricity
Save the environment, walk or bike to school instead of the car
Save the environment, recycle your rubbish
Respect the environment
Save the environment, use your shopping bag again
Save the environment
Use both sides of the paper
Save the environment
Plant your own fruit and veg
Respect the environment
The environment is in danger
Save the environment.

Rebecca Fitzgerald (11)
Pakefield Middle School, Pakefield

I Love My Cats

I love Molly because she is cute
I love Molly because she has kittens
I love Molly because she is loveable.

I love Maisie because she is young
I love Maisie because she is sweet
I love Maisie because she is gorgeous
I love Maisie because she is beautiful.

I love them both because they are better than none.
I love them both because they are cool
I love them both because they are cute
I love them both because they are mine.

Charlotte Winchester (11)
Pakefield Middle School, Pakefield

Me . . .

I am a blonde girl, my hair is naturally one big curl,
I'm the height of a 10 year old, but please don't be cold,
I have blue eyes, like the bright sunny skies,
I also wear glasses, but sometimes mess about in classes.

I love to laugh, but sometimes life takes me down a different path,
I have some great best friends, our good time never ends,
I am quite sensitive, however I do have a lot of love to give,
I love to sing and dance, whenever I get the chance.

I enjoyed taking the time, to write this little rhyme,
Hopefully you now know me a bit better,
Having read this little letter.

Charlotte Read (12)
Pakefield Middle School, Pakefield

Just Because

Just because I don't smoke
doesn't mean that I'm not cool.

Just because I don't fight
doesn't mean that I'm not as hard as anyone else.

Just because I'm not a class clown
doesn't mean that I'm a geek.

Just because I'm quiet
doesn't mean I'm a loser.

Just because I can't play football
Doesn't mean I'm a good at nothing.

Connor Molloy (12)
Pakefield Middle School, Pakefield

Knife News

Every day I come home from school
I see the news
I call it the knife news because all I see is body bags and blood
My mum looks away from the TV but I carry on watching
For these who died when innocent.

Every day I come home from school
I see the news
I see weapons in bodies and families crying
I see victims and murderers and others alike
I carry on watching and count the deaths
That's why I call it the knife news.

Sebastian Mills (12)
Pakefield Middle School, Pakefield

Dear Members Of My Generation

It is bad for you and you could die or could develop asthma
Smoking is a killer . . .

You know it too!
It's not cool to smoke
so don't think it's a joke
to be like friends
make this where it ends!
Stop smoking forever
And say smoking - *never!*
From a friend.

April Taylor (11)
Pakefield Middle School, Pakefield

I Am Me

Just because I will not smoke doesn't mean I'm not cool.
Just because I'm crazy doesn't mean you can say it with me.
Just because I'm mad doesn't mean you need to know
Just because I'm mad doesn't mean you cannot hang with me.
Just because I am me doesn't mean you can rub it in.
Just because I have a bum chin doesn't mean you can rub it in.
I'm Marcus, accept me or not.
I am who I am I will be me forever
I do not care what others think of me
Like me or not that is your choice, accept me for who I am.

Marcus Cruse (11)
Pakefield Middle School, Pakefield

Whale Hunting

Big monsters, bigger than boats
Big monsters, bigger than planes
But they do no harm, yet we do lots of harm to them.
We ram them with our boats, we harpoon them
and we shoot them.
We do all of this so we can have shampoo,
hair brushes and many other things
But soon the whales will all be gone
So we will not have these things
So we must stop killing the whales.

Lewis Rose (11)
Pakefield Middle School, Pakefield

It's Not My Fault

It's not my fault I'm dumb, it doesn't make you brainy
It's not my fault you think you're it
It's not my fault I have no friends, it doesn't mean you have loads.
It's not my fault you say I'm 4 eyes, it doesn't make you 2 eyes
It's not my fault I'm really tall, it doesn't make me fat
Why do it, it doesn't make you tough.

Ben Mann (12)
Pakefield Middle School, Pakefield

128

Just Because

Just because I am Chinese, doesn't mean my English is bad.
Just because I am bad at geography, doesn't mean I hate geography.
Just because my brother is good at sport,
doesn't mean I'm good at sport too.
Just because I am fat, doesn't mean I eat lots.
Just because I am tall, doesn't mean I can fight.
Just because my history is bad, doesn't mean I didn't study.
Just because the teacher is kind,
doesn't mean I need to pass up the homework.
I will be myself forever.

Chiang Chicheng Jasmine (12)
Pakefield Middle School, Pakefield

Why Say It?

Saying I'm dumb, doesn't make you smart,
Saying I'm fat, doesn't make you skinny,
Saying I'm a loser, doesn't make you a winner,
Saying I'm ugly, doesn't make you pretty,
So why say it?
Saying I need to get a life, doesn't make your life any happier,
Saying I'm a teacher's pet, doesn't make the teachers like you,
Saying I'm a geek, doesn't make you cool,
Saying I've got no friends, doesn't make you have more friends,
So why say it?

Molly Spring (13)
Pakefield Middle School, Pakefield

Just Because I'm Ugly?

Just because I'm ugly doesn't mean you're not.
Just because I'm weird doesn't mean you're not.
I am who I am and it can't be changed.
My little sister calls me fat but I know I'm not.
All people are different and it can't be changed.
Some people call me small but it doesn't matter.
Some people lie and they know it's not right.
Just because I'm not your friend doesn't mean that you're mine.
I may be a goodie and you may not.
You are who you are and it can't be changed.

Deni Lipscombe (11)
Pakefield Middle School, Pakefield

Just Because My Mum . . .

Just because my mum is a Muslim doesn't mean I don't love her.
Just because my mum is dark skinned doesn't mean I don't love her.
Just because my mum doesn't go to a Christian church
doesn't mean she doesn't believe which doesn't mean I don't love her.
Just because my mum has spots doesn't mean I don't love her.
Just because my mum isn't good at everything
doesn't mean I don't love her.
Just because my mum is different to every other mum
doesn't mean I don't love her.
She is who she is and she can't be changed.

Iraana Coleman (11)
Pakefield Middle School, Pakefield

I Like My Dog

I like my dog Maizy because she's cute
I like my dog Maizy because she's small
I like my dog Maizy because she loves me
I like my dog Maizy because she's crazy
I like my dog Maizy because she listens to me
I like my dog Maizy because she's good on the lead
I like my dog Maizy because she's cool
I like my dog Maizy because she is good
I like my dog Maizy because she's house trained.

Ben Sharpe (11)
Pakefield Middle School, Pakefield

Drunks

Drunks, they're all the same,
us children are always getting the blame
for messing up our streets
they go past our houses ranting and raving
while drunk, being sick all over the paving.
No one can stop them apart from themselves
but they get too drunk to know what they're doing.
they wake up my street until they move to the next
but all they want to do is get drunk.

Phillippa Dwyer (11)
Pakefield Middle School, Pakefield

Global Warming

The Earth is heating and melting the ice,
More water is appearing,
In a few more years
England might be underwater!
So stop green house gases and help the environment,
Recycle and stop smoking.
We could all do our bit to help this world.
So we will be here for longer!

Katie Varney (11)
Pakefield Middle School, Pakefield

Why Kill Snakes?

What is wrong with the world?
Why kill snakes?
What have they done wrong
apart from the food they take?
What's wrong with snakes?
Why don't you cease?
Just let the snakes
live in peace.

Brandon Renforth (12)
Pakefield Middle School, Pakefield

What's Wrong?

You say I'm fat, well what's wrong with that?
You say I'm too tall, what's wrong? You're small!
You say I'm too big, what's wrong? You're a twig!
You say I've got an ugly mole, what's wrong, shut your cake hole!
You say I think I'm hard, I'm not, doesn't mean you are, what's wrong?
You say I'm weak, what's wrong, you're a geek!
You say do I want a fight, what's wrong, I'll knock out your lights.

Joe Carway (12)
Pakefield Middle School, Pakefield

The Fires Of June

I stand on a precipice,
Gone are thoughts,
Gone are sounds,
Nothing but the chill of silence awaits.

It was not always so,
Once we were joy,
Our laughter filling the heavens,
No longer we play,
Our times moved on, cut through,
An electric flash of never-ending words,
Thoughts dance but cannot be caught.

Reminiscence, should have done more,
Too late now for the body turned to ash,
Yet into the fire we must endure.

Pencil daggers clutched in fists,
Voices murmur, but I hear them not,
Ice knives in my heart,
Red-hot panic threatens to boil.

A figure suspended in gloom points the way,
Through the protruding gates march we on,
Lined in rows we meet our fate,
Be it hapless glory,
Or nought but the crumbling dust,
Dredged in a world that takes none but the best,
Forsworn we'll labour on,
For the ticking must end,
Spots left blank, rife with frustration,
We sit for once not a word takes flight,
Upon the paper reads 12th June,
Exam.

Eleanor Ruffels (15)
Queen Elizabeth's Grammar School, Faversham

The Passing

I sat and watched my grandfather die,
Slumped in a chair of rotting wood.
In the final moments his eyes flickered open,
And followed me, swiftly, as I stood.

'Boy,' he croaked his voice all wrecked,
'Stay for a while longer.
Your presence stirs in me an urge to speak -
And my thoughts grow steadily stronger.'

'That's right,' he sighed, as I sat myself,
By the man and the dying fire.
I leaned in close, as he prepared to start,
And I adhered to his desire.

'Now boy, sit well and listen hard,
For what I will tell you is sad but true.
I shall tell you the story of my grandfather's death -
This may be of interest to you.

For me and him, through thick and thin,
Were fond of each other, dearly.
Then one night he asked something of me -
Oh lad, I remember it clearly.

But before I tell you what it was
My beloved grandpa said,
I wish to tell you how he looked,
Before I left him dead.

Indeed it was a sorry sight
That I wish I could forget.
His face was spent and haggard,
And his eyes were shrunk and wet.

His hair was dry and wispy,
And was falling out in clumps.
I admit, it made me feel ashamed
Of what he had become.

It was a dreary night in late November,
And the room was bitter cold.
Much as it is right now, my lad -
This is what he told:

'Listen you well now, bright-eyed child,
With your head so full of dreams.
Take this blade, and with it -
Tear me at the seams.

For my life is but a burden
On the ones I hold so dear.
I sit here now in constant pain -
Please do it now! Right here!'

And what was I to do, my lad?
It broke my heart to see him so.
For it seemed to me a sweet release,
And he was surely dead in soul.

As dusk descended, I slit his throat,
By the light of the dying ember.
But little did I know, I damned my own soul,
On the accused night in November.

For there is no peace for a killer -
No remorse for this treacherous sin,
The feeling of guilt and sorrow
Cause an atrocious din.

This is all I have for you, boy
But heed this old man's warning:
To take a life is to take your own
Remember it in your mourning.'

Having finished his speech, my grandfather slumped
Back in his rotting chair.
A stir of wind marked his passing,
And whistled through his hair.

As I leant forward, reaching out my hand
To close his staring eyes
It seemed to me that from his throat
Came a string of haunted sighs.

So as if his fatal warning
Should fail to suffice
I was now stuck with this freakish noise -
The price he paid to take a life.

For now I realise, to do such a thing,
And keep it locked inside
Will curse you - now, here and after,
And till death it will reside.

Ronnie Simmonds (17)
Queen Elizabeth's Grammar School, Faversham

Hero In Red

Her boyfriend would come home with it first,
the red, angry burning red.
Then he'd give it to her - my mother.
　　　　Victim at first, but the red
　　　　changes you, she's got it now.

My turn.
It's deeper now, white-hot snowball
growing as it approaches me.

You've found me, pound me
I cry, I cry out
A game of pain
Shame came.
My red instead.

Unbeatable beats the beatable

The red is mine to give out.
No.

I'm going to save you all.
I'll keep the red.
I'll give it to me again and again,
now and then . . . then again . . .
I deserve this, I can control this, this is mine,
this is it, I am your hero.
　　　　This is my red.

Anna Rose Foster (18)
Queen Elizabeth's Grammar School, Faversham

136

Letting Go

It's hard to keep living
With this pain that I'm feeling
'Cause my heart has died
Left out in the rain
Waiting for you to come home tonight.

Though I know it's not right
I wish, I dream, I hope
One more night,
One more minute,
One last breath.

Now these tears won't stop
And I'm feeling a heartache
So strong, I can't bear
To dwell on those memories
Of when you were there.

Nor you or I were to blame
When God willed you couldn't stay
It was your time to go
You could shine no longer
Like we did
When we were younger.

Sent to save me
You return to your place
On God's right side
With angels surrounding.

In my heart you are
And there you'll stay
Day after day
Till time passes away.

Ana Mafalda Guimaraes (15)
Queen Elizabeth's Grammar School, Faversham

My Dog Ate My Grandma's Breakfast

My dog ate my grandma's breakfast -
She did, you know, it's true!
She gobbled down that breakfast
While Granny was on the loo!
Then she crept from the crime scene quietly,
As quietly as she could go
And feigned surprise at the uproar
From Granny, down below.
And came with us back to the crime scene,
To see what it was all about,
And listen to our suspicions
Then dispel us of our doubts.
The innocent eyes were flawless -
'Eggs and bacon? No!
You didn't think *I* did, surely?
I wouldn't sink so low!'

The act was very convincing,
Better than one in a play -
But the toast crumbs in her beard,
Kind of gave her away!

Lucy Carney (14)
Queen Elizabeth's Grammar School, Faversham

The Fox

The fox crept stealthily,
Through the long dry grass,
Then in one flash of orange,
He pounced and caught
His unlucky prey.

A tender young rabbit hung,
Limp in his powerful jaws,
Dead and delicious to eat,
He dribbled and licked his lips,

His ears pricked up alert, at noises around him,
His face alighted with pleasure,
He devoured it happily,
Enjoying its meaty taste.

Bethany Pihama (11)
Queen Elizabeth's Grammar School, Faversham

Love Beginnings

Wind gently caresses the grass,
Love like the wind,
Heart like a path
Roaming through the depths of her soul.
Wondering whether I'll ever get home
I'd rather spend my life with her,
A curse or a blessing, I give not a care,
For she is my loved one, my only,
A fool, me, my brand.
As usual I found the sacred one,
My saviour, the redeemer of my faith.
Slowly I gathered up my pace,
An introduction was all it took,
For a love story, it seemed, a fluke.
Digits we exchanged,
Little did we know, our lives would be changed
Time has tested our eternal bond.
A token of gratitude, a love song,
She strikes a stunning pose,
Ironically she holds the name Rose.
Promises were made,
An oath I willingly swore,
To cherish and adore forever more.
My friends enduringly ponder,
Whom do I sincerely trip over,
My response is a Rose,
And upon my heart is she a tattoo,
My allegiance renewed.
My sweetest taboo.

Juanita Tsikata (16)
St John's Catholic Comprehensive School, Gravesend

Torture Island

Torture island, a horrid and unwanted place to be . . .

I can hear screams as loud as an elephant's roar.

I can see skulls on burning spikes with flames around them like someone is expecting me.

My heart pumps as fast as a cheetah, sprinting for her prey.
In a few minutes, I feel like my heart is going to jump out and burst into the bitter, cold air and try to escape.
The smell is rotten; I can smell dead rats fused with rotten eggs.
The smell is rushing to my head; not even my blood can cope with it.

I feel dead.

Dead as a dead duck with little but thirsty maggots sucking onto the flesh of that unfortunate duck . . .
I can taste the merciless air; it tastes very aboriginal and also tastes worse than an ill child being sick in a cup and forced to drink.
My head feels very confused and feels so big that if I fall down, it will cause a crack in the ground . . .

In addition to this, small but blood-thirsty crows are hovering above my head like they are watching my every move, waiting for a time to strike.

When I try to touch the ground, it feels like knives were held out; the tip of the knife splintering and slashing onto my rough skin, causing it to bleed.

It is too much, the screams, the smell, the taste and the features.
The sooner I taste fresh air and freedom, the better for myself and anyone who dares to walk upon the ground of Torture Island.

Daniel Mosaid (14)
St John's Catholic Comprehensive School, Gravesend

My Hero

My hero is my grandad
Because he's very cool
He died before I knew him
Maybe in a pool.
He was a famous director,
He made lots of money
He certainly wasn't poor
But maybe a bit funny.
In World War 2
He lost his shoe
And became a prisoner of war
His ship blew up
He broke his cup
And saved Lord Forte's life.
They became great friends
Forever and ever
Luckily no one pulled the lever.
I love my grandad Mario Zampi,
He looks like he likes scampi.
So he must be a Zampi,
Like me.

Adelaide Zampi (11)
St Joseph's College, Ipswich

Michael Jackson

My hero is Michael Jackson
Even though he's dead his music still rocks me to sleep in my bed.
If I met him I would probably faint,
He's so great people called him a saint.
My feelings for Michael are happy and sad,
Although some people thought he was bad.
I listen to his music because it is cool,
And then when he sings people think he's no fool.
When the Jackson Five's music started to thrive
The whole world came alive.
And that is why I admire him!

Alex Rudkin (11)
St Joseph's College, Ipswich

A Madman

My hero is a madman!
He sings in town and jumps around
He just doesn't stop messing around
Do you know who he is?
Yes my dad Jasper
He's funny and jumpy
But grumpy and humpy.
He always goes large
Throwing parties and pies.
But I love my dad for the way he is
But come on he doesn't have to be a twit
He plays jokes and hides things when you need them
He is like a baby or maybe a kid.
He always changes the channel,
What an annoying trouble,
My dad is awesome.
He likes to think he's Elvis
But he can't do the pelvis
And it's always a laugh when he has left the building
My dad is wicked
How about yours?

Jacob David Dormer (11)
St Joseph's College, Ipswich

My Heroine

My sister is my heroine
I'll bet you're wondering why?
She's sweet, she's kind, she makes me smile . . .
But sometimes she just . . .
Blows my mind!
I couldn't live without her because
I love her so much!
But if there's one thing that makes me
proud of her is that she's such a fighter
and never ever doubts me.

Georgia Stark (11)
St Joseph's College, Ipswich

143

Future

Arms open wide,
Run for the pride,
Calling my name,
Waiting for fame.
One day one day,
I'll make it I pray,
Exhilarating feelings,
Ecstatic beings.
I know I will be there,
All the way to see yer.
In the future I can do it,
Get all the way through it.
So off I go,
On the road to hi ho,
To be in the future,
Something worthwhile,
As long as you're happy,
You can never be trashy,
On the road in my life,
I will carry on I'm sure.

Matthew Watling (11)
St Joseph's College, Ipswich

Feelings

When people tease me, I feel rather down,
I feel like I could never stifle my frown.

When people please me, I feel phenomenally ecstatic,
But please do not confuse me with a fanatic.

When these exceptionally wondrous feelings arouse,
The worried fires of my conscience automatically douse.

I feel that I'll never go through life with density,
I'll never go through life with a single complexity.

James Battye (11)
St Joseph's College, Ipswich

My Heroic Hero

My hero's heroic
He wins tons of tennis tournaments
He is strong with tons of muscle on him
I wish I was that strong
I even copied his hairstyle
But not quite so long
Have you guessed who it is?
Yes it is
Nadal the great
Well he is to me anyway
I even like the same court as him
Clay court, Rolland Garros to be precise
They have the best courts
But hey, let's get back to my hero
Nadal
He is my real hero.

Antonio Capasso (11)
St Joseph's College, Ipswich

My Heroes

My heroes are funny
They are like children at times
One acts like a child all the time
They are loving and caring
As they do so much for me
I am very glad I've got them
Have you guessed who they are?
Well they're my mum and dad
I feel I've got the best parents in the world
They're wonderful people and they would never ever let us get hurt
They are always there for me
If one of them leaves a part of me will die!
They will never leave my heart as they will sit there and stay
We've been through ups and down
Our down was when my uncle Malcolm died
That killed me and I will never fill that chip in my heart.

Lois Scott (11)
St Joseph's College, Ipswich

My Grandad

My grandad is my hero
Even though I can never meet him
My dad speaks of him like a king
As he saved lives he is more important to me than
any sportsman or actor.
Heroes aren't made overnight, they are born
I have a lump in my throat when I talk about him
If I met him all my sadness would rush away
He would leave me speechless
So no words can describe him
Only he can describe himself.
I hear him in the night calling my name and I get sad.
Then I think about what a great man he was
An astonishing person
He's my hero.

Philip Dowding-Young (12)
St Joseph's College, Ipswich

Harry Ellis The Hero

Harry Ellis
Harry Ellis the hero,
He's the Harry from Heaven.
He wins the game and scores the tries.
He makes set plays and
He does, yes, he plays every game.
He's the man,
the man to interview,
the man to watch,
and the man to play,
He will hit them hard
and he likes to say . . .
'Come on England!'
He must be,
Yes, he's Harry Ellis.

George Williams (11)
St Joseph's College, Ipswich

Grandad

My grandad was amazing
He was always there for me
I was nine when he died
I still think of him daily
He made me who I am today
He's my one and only.

He would always make me laugh
And draw with me in the cellar
He is the father of my dad
He was a wonderful fella
We would run around and always play
Every minute of every day.

He is my grandad and always will be
Even if he's not here with me.

Georgie East (11)
St Joseph's College, Ipswich

My Grandad

My grandad is my hero
It's not my friend, he's at school
He let me build a jet plane
OK, it was quite small
I got to break a window
In fact I broke two
My grandad's car
And the house too
But he still loves me.

Lindsay Hammond Smith (12)
St Joseph's College, Ipswich

My Brother

I love my brother
As he always looks out for me
Makes sure I'm safe
When he went to the army
I lost a part of me
Every time he comes home
That part comes back
Every time I see him
He makes me feel happy.

Clarice Elise Bickers (12)
St Joseph's College, Ipswich

Jonny Wilkinson

Jonny is the game,
Jonny is the name,
His kicks make me proud,
And in 2003 he made England loud,

His tackles are supreme,
To play like him would be my dream,
He is just amazing,
And his name is totally crazy!

Jonny Renshaw (11)
St Joseph's College, Ipswich

Alastair Cook

My idol is amazing at cricket,
He's a really nice guy,
He opens the batting for England,
He's scored 9 test hundreds,
He makes me feel;
Joyful, excited, astonished and
Proud to be English!
His name is Alastair Cook!

Sam Chapman (12)
St Joseph's College, Ipswich

Rivers Flow

Rivers flow through the dust
Rivers flow through the banks
Rivers flow with rage they must
Many times they just rush.

Dust travels at the speed of light
Dust travels every night
Dust travels at every height
Many times they rush.

Rocks move through the sea
Rocks move against me
Rocks move through the key
Many times they rush.

Alice Clement (12)
St Neots Community College, Eynesbury

My Lover

When I see the right boy
I know he's the one for me
Whenever I see him
I fill up with glee

He's caring and he's cute
He's just the one for me
I love him I love him
Wedding bells it will be.

Chloe-Anne Flint (12)
St Neots Community College, Eynesbury

My Family

I wouldn't be without them,
They keep me safe and sound,
I wouldn't change my family,
I love having them around.

My family, my family,
They mean the world to me,
Mum, Dad, and little Ben,
And then that just leaves me.

Chloe Gibson (11)
St Neots Community College, Eynesbury

Cupid

Heart warmer,
Arrow shooter,
Loving wings,
Natural bonder,
Fate decider,
Love invader,
Friendship developer.

Danielle Lewell (11)
St Neots Community College, Eynesbury

Him

He was a tiger in battle
he was as fast as lightning
he leapt like a frog
he was as humble as Jesus
he was as clever as Stephen Hawking
he was as fat as a pig
he was as calm as a Buddha
that person . . .
Was . . .
Him.

Camen Singh Mahli (13)
Sir Joseph Williamsons Mathematical College, Rochester

School Days

On Monday everything's boring
We have PE this morning
With our new teachers snoring
Mondays are so boring
Even I feel like snoring

On Tuesday all is long
All the kids feel wrong
Our playground will pong
Tuesdays are so long
Even I feel like snoring

On Wednesday the weather is cool
Our teacher is so cool
We get to dive in the pool
The weather is so cool
But still I feel like snoring

On Thursday all is good
And everything really should
I know they really would
There's only one day left
Why should I snore

On Friday it's so splendid
School has finally ended
Plus we're not suspended
On Friday school ends
I would not dare snore.

William Turner
Sir Joseph Williamsons Mathematical College, Rochester

The Clown

We went to the circus at 2 o'clock,
but when we got there, we were in for a shock.
There were jugglers, acrobats and fire-eaters too,
the floor was filled with elephant doo-doo,
but none could compete with my favourite part,
for they were the clowns, and that was an art,
he came out with his spotty baggy trousers on,
singing a silly stupid, little song,
his large shiny nose stuck out of his face,
then he hopped on a spacehopper and had a little race,
with himself, of course, just for laughs,
and then he called out, 'Time for baths!'
he pulled out a bucket of God knows what,
but from up in the balcony, he looked like a dot,
he did some more acts including ladders and chairs,
but I couldn't help looking at his red fluffy hairs.
you could obviously see it was a wig,
his shoes were huge, ginormous and big,
when we went home I had a smile on my face,
and I will always remember that spacehopper race.
I will always remember that dodgy smile,
it would make anyone run a mile,
except me, because I love clowns,
so I ran all the way home in leaps and bounds.

Reece Hannaford (12)
Sir Joseph Williamsons Mathematical College, Rochester

Edmund Of The Nightly Glade

Once upon a haunted night,
There sat in his miserable house,
Edmund of the Nightly Glade,
feeding a lonely mouse.
Edmund's sister, Ms Baptista,
Once went to visit,
but finding that he was gone,
She checked all of the drawers,
Wondering, where on Earth is he?
She ran past windows and doors,
Then she wept,
but the search she kept.
Though many a year later,
Most people do hate her,
She visited him once again more,
and found no trace,
but a vast empty space.
At last she reached his dreaded study,
And there in the corner of the
darkened room, highlighted by a
Ghastly glow, stood he.
Edmund, never to be more.

Samu Siltanen-Tinsley (12)
Sir Joseph Williamsons Mathematical College, Rochester

I Just Wanna Die

Monday: I go to my 'pen-pushers' job,
It was different this time; I met a gang of yobs.
One threw a missile at me, it really hurt you see,
I head outside for my coffee break - and get stung by a bee!

Tuesday: I get paid hurray! It's my lucky day!
£413 and some bills; I'll just throw the bills away.
I rush home to my wife, showing her the dosh,
She recognises the little amount; her reaction was, 'Oh gosh.'

Wednesday: I pop round the bar, pull out a cigar,
Some youths grab hold of me and take me very far.
'Where's the dosh mate?' I hear someone say,
So I practice some Kung-Fu moves and technically fly away!

Thursday: rain, rain, go away,
Come again on Saturday,
That will put a massive stop . . .
To Man U's chances of going to the top.

Friday: office is hot and I am sweaty,
The papers are torn like confetti.
I talk to one colleague, he tells me to go away,
I am shocked and speechless; I don't know what to say!

Liam Martin-Lane (13)
Sir Joseph Williamsons Mathematical College, Rochester

Debris Flew Everywhere

The car zoomed past me,
I felt the world turn,
In the distance I saw it,
The Lambo,
Did a 180°,
It was heading straight for me,
The door opened,
I had to jump in,
So when the opportunity came I did,
My dream car embraced me,
The driver yelled,
'Get ready!'
I didn't have time,
The car accelerated past 200mph,
I felt my face vacuum,
An oncoming car was ahead,

. . .

Debris flew everywhere.

Jordan Michael Bryant (12)
Sir Joseph Williamsons Mathematical College, Rochester

The Unknown

Darkness, truly do we fear it
Yes, you may think it true,
but I know different.
No, it is not the darkness we fear,
but the unknown.
For we know not what lurks in the darkness, in the shadows.
Death may wait for us,
yet irrational, our fear may be,
pleasant things may await us.
But truly, we know not what stalks us,
in the shadows,
the darkness,
the unknown.

Akshay Singh (12)
Sir Joseph Williamsons Mathematical College, Rochester

The Underworld

The underworld dark and lame
The place where the dead come to stay
Tortures are created by the Greek god Hades
And by his side sits the fates

Cerberus, Cerberus the dog with 3 heads
Guards the gates of Hades
As the ghosts zoom by
No living things passing by

Elysium fields, the isles of the blessed
The places you go if you lived a hero's life
But if you've been cruel, killed, or cursed
You will end up in Tarterus

Remember to not be a sinner
Or in death your life will be grimmer
So prey to the Gods and Zeus on high
And he will protect you from the humans' worst crime.

Mitchal Pine (13)
Sir Joseph Williamsons Mathematical College, Rochester

Zombini

They were out walking at a really bad time,
But it wasn't humans committing the crime.
Creatures started emerging, from under the ground,
To stalk the humans as they walked around.
They walked and walked hunting you down,
But no one did realise that it was Bini the clown!
He had gone totally mad,
Thinking about what it had.
There had been blood on the walls,
On the stairs and in the halls,
You could never escape,
You'd be gone at the drop of his cape,
And since he was dead,
Killed in his bed,
He'll never be able to leave!

Connor Fitzgerald (12)
Sir Joseph Williamsons Mathematical College, Rochester

The Simpsons

Homer is a big, fat lazy bum
He eats all day and weighs a tonne.
He has his butt-groove in his couch,
He is mainly a slouch.

Bart is a super-wiz on his skateboard,
He can ollie over the biggest Ford.
In school he is everyone's favourite class-clown,
He is always getting his sister down.

Lisa is very smart and is a nerd,
She is always doing science experiments on birds.
She is a legend on the sax,
Her favourite drink is Pepsi Max.

Maggie is a little baby who likes her toys,
She is not too keen on boys.
She likes playing with her dummies,
Her teacher is Mr Lumly.

Liam William Hammond (12)
Sir Joseph Williamsons Mathematical College, Rochester

The Trenches

I stood there frozen at the sight I saw,
Hundreds of bodies littered the floor,
the noises of battle filled my head,
all the diplomatic words were said,
the gunshots still echoing through the field,
they shot, they killed,
how I survived I don't know,
the fear in me began to grow,
I had to get out of here,
then the gun in my pocket grew ever near,
I pulled the trigger,
I no longer have a figure.

Thomas Judge (12)
Sir Joseph Williamsons Mathematical College, Rochester

Special Places

The mountain was there
Sitting there in its beauty
My one special place

The great blue ocean
The water shimmering lightly
My one special place

The Saharan plain
The clouds floating over me
My one special place

I went straight under
Fishes swimming around me
My one special place

The huge Amazon
Apes swinging from the trees
My one special place.

Liam Mattingly (13)
Sir Joseph Williamsons Mathematical College, Rochester

Polly Cat

My cat Polly has stood a lot of things,
having sore whiskers and getting bee stings,
having a scratched tail and going to the vet,
getting her claws stuck in our swingball set,
protecting her territory from other cats,
torturing all the little mice and rats,
eating her food while you're still serving it,
finding some quite awkward places to sit,
eating the sausage that we have with our chips,
squinting her eyes and licking her lips,
sleeping in my wardrobe and putting fluff on my tops,
sitting on the road while we go to the shops,
telling her, 'Come into the house,' when it's foggy,
I adore my cat, she's one lovely moggy.

Megan Bailes (12)
Stalham High School, Stalham

Photographs

You hold the past in your hands
You see your friends again
You see your loved ones
You see weird places
And the most amazing things
The things that shock you
Black and white, sepia
Great effects that make you smile
Or make you upset.

Beth Younge (15)
Stalham High School, Stalham

12 Strong Men

I
headed
12 strong men
into the east
bronze and glittering
serving in the air fleet
water under the bridge now!
several missions, several medals.

William Richardson (12)
Stalham High School, Stalham

Nintendo

Play,
Download,
Anywhere.
What a touch screen!
What game shall we play?
If I ever lost it
I would cry and cry and cry!

Jacob Surgenor (11)
Stalham High School, Stalham

The Egg Or The Chicken?

There's nothing that can heal the terror,
Nothing that will get rid of the fear,
When innocent blood has been spread by
2 teenagers high on their head,
Holding their guns
Walking into school
Killing countless students,
And a teacher too.
Why did they do it?
Why spill innocent blood?
And most of all who's to blame for it all?
The school?
The teachers?
The students?
The parents?
Most point the blame on music and clothes
But isn't it the parents job to stay home?
One was taking anti-depressive drugs
While the other had a messed up
Mind, counting suicide.
Journals they wrote in,
Spilling out their dark thoughts
But the anti-depressant drugs didn't stop them,
Nothing could.
They were being bullied it's true but
Why turn their guns on the school?
After the massacre, after the blood,
They committed suicide,
As they said they would.
And even as they are dead the
Horror continues,
Horrible world.
Mad world.
Where the number of dead rises every second,
So who came first the egg or the chicken?

Ruffa Kemp (12)
Stowmarket Middle School, Stowmarket

Red Cattle

Sugar, apparently
is bad for our teeth
But what then happens
when we look underneath
all the beef
we eat today
Is that much better
would you say?
Sure it gives you
a longer-lasting boost
but what does it give the Earth?
All it does is introduce
another factor
to the growing ozone layer
are the cows the ones to blame?
No they are not the slayer
of the land of the world
Surely McDonald's are
to blame
for producing so much methane
a deadly gas that will kill us
all one day
so leave the cows alone
I say.
It's our fault the world's going astray.

Lucy Ramsden (13)
Stowmarket Middle School, Stowmarket

Graffiti

Walking down the streets of town,
Passing each and every shop,
Until you turn around the corner,
Then your eyes go pop.

Then on the wall in front of you,
And on the floor as well,
Lie the leftovers of spray cans,
But who should you tell?

You then leave the site,
With the image in your head,
And for the rest of the day,
It stays until you go to bed!

This is something that happens each day,
To someone unexpecting,
As they walk around the corner,
Our walls need protecting.

Hannah Lockwood (12)
Stowmarket Middle School, Stowmarket

Untitled

Drugs and alcohol make us crazy,
And afterwards they make us lazy,
Drugs can make you high as a kite,
So can alcohol, even WKD lite.
Just like Michael Jackson's Thriller,
People get a kick out of being a killer,
Dirty girls lying in the gutter,
Boys walking around, shouting like nutters,
Night by night, day by day,
Homeless people waste away,
All the things we see today,
Sitting down the alleyway,
Sad things are all around,
Lying there, waiting to be found.

Jessica Smith (12)
Stowmarket Middle School, Stowmarket

Dark Nights And Blind Minds

Quietly creeping down the street,
Nowhere near as being neat,
In their big bold hoodies,
They are the bad buddies.

Blocking every alley in sight,
In millions and millions of fights,
Drunken and hazy all the time,
In conclusion there's loads of crime.

Damaged but coloured walls,
Empty spray cans on the stone floor,
The light dim as can be,
You can hardly see.

Falling and strolling all around,
Homeless, waiting to be found,
Wanting to kill,
While some are saying their last will.

Cansu Aslan (12)
Stowmarket Middle School, Stowmarket

Going Back To The War

Although the credit crunch may get you down,
there is no need to wear a frown.
People are really feeling the hit,
so we need to get those candles lit.
Lots think it is getting worse,
they think it's become a daily curse.
But if we go back to the war,
money was really going out the door.
Because of rationing, there was a lack of food,
but many still stayed in a cheerful mood.
We should follow the trend that they set,
without the tiniest regret.
So if you're at home thinking everything's lost its sparkle,
think of them.

Chelsea Voller (13)
Stowmarket Middle School, Stowmarket

In This Age

More problems are everywhere,
More people's cupboards are bare.
Things are getting so much worse,
No more money in your purse.

People are sinking further down,
Worse and worse becomes their frown,
More and more lose their jobs,
People grumble and sigh and sob.

But even though you may feel down,
There's no need to wear a frown,
Everything's worthwhile,
Just to give a smile!

Leah Smalley (12)
Stowmarket Middle School, Stowmarket

The Credit Crunch Crisis

We hear every day on the news,
of lots subjects which put you in the blues.
'The credit crunch is here!' screams the press,
people's money is getting less and less.
Everyone's smiles are turned to frowns,
all of them are feeling down.
Every day people lose their jobs,
it makes them all want to moan and sob.
When is this non-stop crisis going to end?
The banks have nothing left to lend.
Food prices are rising day by day,
Why can't the credit crunch just go away?

Hannah Mayhew (12)
Stowmarket Middle School, Stowmarket

Don't Blame Us!

We see on the news, and hear on the radio,
They talk about teens committing crimes in the studios.
We are stereotyped for all the wrong reasons,
We commit crimes through all the seasons.
But are we to blame?
We don't make the immortal video games.
Or the drugs and alcohol that damages our physiques,
All of those make us ill and incomplete.
Hoodies are the fashion, not a threat,
Maybe people shouldn't make accusations and forget.
So don't blame us, it's not our fault,
Talk to the older folks who accuse for assault.

Chloe Lynch (12)
Stowmarket Middle School, Stowmarket

Who Me?

I am eating my breakfast and I hear on the telly
A child was abused with bruises and cuts,
My mum said the parents ought to pull up their socks
I am really lucky my parents don't mock.
Children get abused every day,
The shock made me need a long lay.
I really don't know why peoples think it's us.
It's not like any of us make a fuss.
We are not even old enough to drive a bus.
We are young and don't have children,
Accuse the older ones who have abused and damaged.

Lauren Cogman (12)
Stowmarket Middle School, Stowmarket

Dirty Drugs

Drugs are all about these days,
but listen to what the policeman says,
Don't waste your time on these,
because they're just not the bee's knee.

People try these lifetime killers,
but they just end up with their heads on pillows.
You may say drugs can do good and bad,
though for some reason we always hear about the sad.

So what is the moral of this?
To give bad drugs a bye-bye kiss!

Sarah Rodwell (12)
Stowmarket Middle School, Stowmarket

Money Worries

Although your money may be low,
Soon a money tree may grow.
Do we blame all the banks,
And shoot them down with tanks?
All these money worries,
We might end up eating curries!
We use money in every day life,
The people up top are slicing it with a knife.
How do we turn our money problems round?
Save each and every little pound!

Elizabeth Gray (12)
Stowmarket Middle School, Stowmarket

The Crazy Generation

iPod Nanos and TVs, many teens love these,
Cigarettes and WKD, these make people crazy.
Things so sweet, make me tweet,
Drugs and vomiting is what you see.

Although the credit crunch has bombed Britain,
We're still managing to keep kittens.
Poor young babies, men losing ladies,
We're making chains of daisies.

I know . . .

Rachel Smythe (13)
Stowmarket Middle School, Stowmarket

Endless Love War

Love feels like war
Me and you are just losing more and more
But every once in a while
Something rekindles our smile,
There's a glimmer of hope,
And we both grab a hold of the rope,
We climb the rope to its prime,
But it only lasts a matter of time,
Before we start to lose our grip,
And we both start to slip,
Falling back through the trapdoor,
Back to how it was before,
I don't think I have the strength to stand much more,
In this endless love war.

Ryan Robert Ingram (15)
Sudbury Upper School, Sudbury

Truest Thoughts

Let me express my truest thoughts, express my truest feelings,
I thought I loved you but now I'm not sure
I thought that when we first started talking our relationship was secure
You assured me it was, but I just couldn't see
How this could ever work, if you didn't love me,
If we could go back to the start, I would
But I've been through too much, so I'm not sure I could.
I thought from here, it got better
But it seems to be getting worse
Like our relationship is in reverse.
We don't talk anymore, I thought we were staying friends
Forget it . . . this break is too big to make amends
Listen to what I'm saying, or I'll leave you feeling despair
These are my truest thoughts and feelings
Flowing through the air.

I thought I loved you, but that all changed
When you jumped on the next man and said it wasn't arranged
I believed you for a moment, I thought I knew you too well for that
It turns out I was wrong because you went behind my back
You asked me to forgive you,
After everything you done to me
Because I can guarantee, that this was the last time,
That you will ever see me, you were just like all the others
There was no change there,
Don't think that you are rare
Because I see you everywhere.

Jordan Pickett (15)
Sudbury Upper School, Sudbury

He's The One

He is tougher than metal,
He is stronger than stone.
You can grab the chance early,
Or sit and let him go.

He's like a brand new Cadillac,
Trust him like your old guitar,
You can run with the moment
Or stay as you are.

So we are going to the surface,
And we are staying where we're heard,
Say you will see him on the other side,
Go find him out of this world.

Abbie Broom (14)
Sudbury Upper School, Sudbury

Winter Spells

The sun disappears and the clouds turn grey
And the wind grows colder day by day.

I go to bed and look outside
I see the colours pass my eyes.

I lay awake and listen to the sounds
Of cold winter rain falling on the ground.

I wake up with a terrible fright,
That all the colours were left with white.

I now know that winter is here,
So everyone give a cheer!

Kirsty Habel (13)
Sudbury Upper School, Sudbury

Spring Is Coming

Flowers blossom in the fresh clean air,
Trees stand tall and bare.

Sun brightening up the sky,
Birds singing as they fly by.

Seagulls sit bobbing up and down,
While I stand watching them in my nice warm gown.

The green grass sways softly in the gentle breeze,
Those fluffy dandelions that make me sneeze.

The church bells in the morning that make a ding,
That is the feel of the oncoming spring.

Kate Hurley (13)
Sudbury Upper School, Sudbury

Grandad

(In memory of Great Grandad, who sadly passed away, on 30/09/08)

You've reached the light at the end of the road
But why did you have to go?
Great Grandad I'll miss you
And never forget the way you
Hugged me when I was upset.
I'll miss you forever, I promise, I will
And never forget you either
But I guess for now is my last goodbye
So, so sorry you had to die.

Rebecca Davidson (13)
Sudbury Upper School, Sudbury

A Dance Of A Lifetime

It really was magical,
Holding him in my arms.

Shame it only lasted a minute
But it was a dance of a lifetime.

I will never forget that night,
That very magical night.

For I will keep that memory,
Until the day I die.

April Jade Clark (14)
Sudbury Upper School, Sudbury

Alone

Alone in the corner
Full of tears to be shed
The one with all the bags
And the pale, pale head
Tatty, old sheets, with rips everywhere
A cardboard box for a shelter from the air
Wanting to be loved
And maybe someone to care
The poor little girl with the bright ginger hair.

Kerri Stowe (14)
Sudbury Upper School, Sudbury

Untitled

Woke up in the morning
When the day was dawning
My mum woke me
To say
Grandad's gone away
I didn't know what to say
I cried and cried
My grandad had died.

Olivia Anderson (13)
Sudbury Upper School, Sudbury

My Grandad

You're like my warmth in the winter,
You're my flower in the autumn,
You're my red-hot in the freezing blue,
Don't leave me please, don't go,
The leaves fly away, I am all alone,
The warmth has gone, I am freezing cold,
Now I stand by your grave,
You left me after all,
My mum said you are watching me, from above.

Lucy Wilson (13)
Sudbury Upper School, Sudbury

Untitled

She's got three crosses, wrote across her hand,
She's got the moonlight, shining down on her now,
She's got all the eyes in the room, looking at her now,
As the cheers go to the stage, go from her now.

H-h-h-her teeth bite down, she's got your last kiss,
Still laying on her lip, she's got your last touch still on her mind
And the lipstick smeared right down on her cheek.

Lydia McKnight (14)
Sudbury Upper School, Sudbury

Summer

Summer is sunny but people make it funny
Playing in the pool and bathing in the sun
All day long in the boiling sun.

Playing with their pets, is what they do best
Enjoying the games they all play together
Bathing in the sun they laugh and shout.
Enjoying the summer is what it's all about.

Debbie Castle (13)
Sudbury Upper School, Sudbury

The Lonely Heart

A cry echoed through her empty mind
Her thoughts, her memories, did unwind.
She slept alone on the cold damp street
Shaking all over from her head to her feet.
Her tears slipped down her old weathered face,
Her lonely heart cried, and she died in this place.

Laura Barnard (13)
Sudbury Upper School, Sudbury

Untitled

Fresh warm air
The heat beaming down on you
The sparkling sea glistening in the light
Swimming in the glistening sea
A nice breeze
Turkey is paradise.

James Spurway (14)
Sudbury Upper School, Sudbury

Oh How I Do Love Being Young

Listen to your iPod,
Work on your laptop,
Talk and text on your phone,
Oh how I love being young.

Going out, having fun,
Staying in and playing games,
Having tea round my friends,
Oh how I love being young.

Going to school is not so cool,
All that work we have to do,
Still it's nearly home time,
Oh how I love being young.

Leah Douglas (11)
Swanley Technology College, Swanley

Young People

Young people are always inside.
Never get out instead they're in house bored and trying to hide.
All they care about is friends and lives.
Some are out carrying blades and knives,
Some are worrying about future ahead.
While others are lazy and lying in bed.
Older ones are with crime and drugs.
While kids are out adventuring and finding bugs.
Most days going to school.
Older ones only try to be cool.
Bunking off and skipping class.
While others working hard and fast.
Sitting at home listening to iPod and phone.
Playing PlayStation which they can't call as their own.
Stealing and crime, there isn't a time.
Older age boring and fine.
My age is better.
Might as well stick with mine.

Megan James (11)
Swanley Technology College, Swanley

It Was That Night, I Didn't Do My Homework

It was that night I didn't do my homework
It was that night that I hated
It wasn't my fault I got distracted
But they took my games away, I almost fainted
Now for a month I can't go and play
No more late nights or eating sweets
I can't do anything, I can't play on the Wii
So now I'm grounded, I can't get any treats
So there you have it, it wasn't my fault
I know who did it,
It was Luke, that boy is so annoying
He can make me puke.

Sam Watkins (12)
Swanley Technology College, Swanley

174

Love Is Life

A boy was dazzled by those red soft lips.
A girl was dazzled by those sparkling eyes.
There's something in life that we call love
And that's what happened to this boy and this girl.

By a train station it was when I saw those red lips
And when I saw those sparkling eyes
I was in love.

We walked towards each other
Then I tripped and dropped my books.
He ran and helped me up
He and I were head over heels.

'Hi, my name's Joe, nice to meet you.'
'Hi, my name's Grace, nice to meet you.'
'I was blown away by those rosy red lips back there.'
'I was blown away by those sparkling eyes back there.'

These were the happiest days of their lives.

Joey Fenner (11)
Swanley Technology College, Swanley

Demons Vs Dragons

Demons teleport in your eyes!
Dragons fly right into the sky!
The demon uses shadow ball!
As the dragon uses fire spin!
While humans were losing!
As I was the one to stop the fight!
But when the demon used light!
Everything was going to burn!
But least it isn't the Earth!
Demons teleported right into the sky!
Dragons flew back when they died!

Wesley Window (11)
Swanley Technology College, Swanley

Small And Helpless

Children, small and helpless,
Their mother always protecting them,
Almost like they care too much, but not enough,
Children like helpless lion cubs in a huge forest.

Children, small and helpless,
Children fly through the field, like a young eagle,
In the sky above, flying home to their mothers,
Snuggling up to their mothers, happy and safe.

Children, small and helpless,
Are said to be seen but never heard,
Listening to adults around them for guidance,
Like a cat and a kitten.

Children, small and helpless,
One day will grow up big and strong,
Like a leader of a pack,
They will one day lead their own.

Emily Whitehead (12)
Swanley Technology College, Swanley

People

Some people think they can't take it anymore
Some people think they are all hardcore
They act like they know it all
And really they know nothing at all!

In my eyes we are all on the same level
Even though some act like the devil
We may not look the same or be the same
But really we are all human!

Lauren Booker (11)
Swanley Technology College, Swanley

Young People Today!

Young people today,
They're always inside,
They should go out and play,
But instead they sit indoors and hide.

There's hopscotch and netball,
There's basketball there's tennis,
So go outside and have some fun,
Don't stay indoors until the day is done.

Back when I was a kid,
There was no computers or PlayStations or phones,
So we made up games,
With sticks and cones.

If we could do it,
So can you,
Don't sit around all day,
Like you're stuck to the chair with glue.

Megan Yuill (11)
Swanley Technology College, Swanley

Crime

Young children read the paper,
In the air crime's around.
When would the crime end?
They should own up that it's them.
Too many dead people because of you out there!

Chloe Everest (11)
Swanley Technology College, Swanley

New Secondary School

The day I've been waiting for,
It's finally here.
We can get up and get ready,
Ready to cheer.

With new shiny shoes,
I'm ready to go.
My uniform's on,
I'm looking just so.

Walking to school,
I'm seriously scared.
Talking to friends,
I feel more prepared.

I had no need to worry,
The day went great.
Can't wait for tomorrow,
I hope I'm not late.

Amy Manning (11)
Swanley Technology College, Swanley

Fade To A Dream

I smile as he drifts by, his soft sweet scent,
I can't help but feel me and him are meant
Why aren't we together? Do you not like how I look?
Am I not the perfect thing you'd find in a film or in a book?
What is this wall between you and me?
Let's break it down so we can be free
As I walk through the corridor and into the hall
You're in there with your friends kicking a ball
I smile as I hurry, rushing past
I want to remove my shy mask
My friend nudges me, 'He smiled back'
I wish I could talk to him but in confidence I lack
'I love you, I love you,' I want to scream
But I'll stay quiet and let it fade to a dream.

Annabel Barratt (13)
Swavesey Village College, Swavesey

Spring

Dappled light through the trees
A robin puffs up his breast
Dawn breaks with a gentle breeze
Newly laid eggs in a nest.

Chinking of milk bottles at the door
The wind ruffles the leaves
Up above the swallows soar
Running in our shirtsleeves.

Sparkly dew in the early morning
The smell of new-mown hay
The stream through the wood contentedly bubbling
A picnic at midday.

Bicycles weaving through the meadow
Kingfishers with rainbow wings
A hideaway in the secret hollow
All the glories of spring.

Blackberries ripening in the hedgerows
All the glories of spring
Standing under the weeping willow
All the glories of spring.

Anna Harris (13)
Swavesey Village College, Swavesey

Teenagers, What Can I Say . . . ?

Teenagers, what can I say?
We stay up all night
And go to school during the day.
Teenagers, what can I say?
We go out shopping and use our parent's money to pay.
Teenagers, what can I say?
We love fizzy drinks and yummy takeaways.
Teenagers, what can I say?
We like to talk, we have a lot to say.
Teenagers, what can I say?

Beth Whelan (14)
Swavesey Village College, Swavesey

I Think We're Quite Cool

Why does everyone treat a teenager like a fool?
When actually I think we are quite cool.
People just need to give us a rest
So we can try and do our best.
Old people blame us all the time
For stupid gun and knife crime.
Old people should get out a bit more
Instead of being such big bores.
They just need to go out and see
Just how good some of us can be.
We can show them what some of us are like
Most of us don't go carrying a knife.
Some people just need to give us a chance.

Isobel Bennett (13)
Swavesey Village College, Swavesey

Love?

How do you know it's real?
Is it a big deal?
Do I love you
Or is it untrue?

If this is love
All of the above
I found you
This has got to be true.

Your eyes are brown
You never frown
You're who I found
You'll always be around.

Georgia Whitbread (13)
Swavesey Village College, Swavesey

Alone In The Playground

As she waits on the playground for someone to come,
Biting her nails and sucking her thumb.
With no one there to give her a hand,
There she will be and alone she will stand.
She's classed as a geek, just because she is bright,
And laughed at because her clothes are not right.
They say she's a loser, with no friends at all,
They say she's a weirdo, and extremely uncool.
Will she ever be able to call them her friends?
It's up to them and so it depends.
Will anyone ever reach out their hand?
Or alone in the playground, is that where she'll stand.

Matilda Perez (13)
Swavesey Village College, Swavesey

Me As A Teen

I'm a teen
Some say I'm mean
I don't go to school because I'm too cool
I wear a hoodie
Don't mean I'm moody
My dad's an alcoholic
He's got a can of beer in his pocket
My mum's a dropout
Don't mean I have to be one.

James Murray (13)
Swavesey Village College, Swavesey

Teenager

The large group of teenagers walked past
Every one of them looking scary
Enough bling for the whole wide world
Not even them would scare me
At the bus stop hanging around
Got to go, the bus was here
Even though they were very scary
Run, they were chasing me!

Ryan Marsh (13)
Swavesey Village College, Swavesey

Conscience

The sun is shining bright in the sky
As the wind passes me by
But then why do they always have to lie
If they get in a fight they might cry
Looking back at her red hair
The gang's got her, it's not fair
She had great blue eyes
But now I am alone with a big sigh.

Callum McDermott (13)
Swavesey Village College, Swavesey

Ghost Of You

The ghost of you is at my door,
It comes each day at twenty past four,
I hoped tonight it wouldn't come,
But at four and twenty-one,

I heard a knocking on the door,
But not at twenty past four,
You were late; you weren't on time,
I wonder where you'd been but mine.

I tugged the door with all my might,
And saw you drenched in summer light,
I clenched you tightly and oh so sadly,
And from then I knew I had to be . . .

'I'm sorry,' you cried, in the summer breeze,
And as I fell upon my knees,
I knew that what we had was gone,
Just like a robin's winter song.

You walked away and left me there,
Lying entrenched in my despair,
But slowly I rose to live again,
And fought my way through the pain.

The ghost of you no longer comes,
No longer haunts from four till one,
I now leave your ghost at my door,
To wait, again, till twenty past four.

Jade Harman (15)
The Phoenix School, Fulbourn

Wanting

Waking up to the sound of darkness in her head,
She screams internally, listens to what is said.
Her mind, casting threats and desires,
Telling her constantly, 'The others are liars'
She arises, secretively, does what is told,
The mystery of this number, waiting to unfold.
The unknown reality ripping her apart,
Her family then trying to pull her own heart,
Towards health . . . but she can't.
The little girl screaming has to stay quiet day by day,
Hoping,
Just praying,
That her thoughts would just,
slowly,
slip,
away.

Madelynn Audreen Hadley (15)
The Phoenix School, Fulbourn

A Friend Is A Friend

Whenever I am alone
I think of you
Talking to you on the phone
I think of you
Playing at the park
I think of you
Or at the disco in the dark
I think of you
When we watched TV
I think of you
You shared secrets with me
I think of you
But when you moved away
I was so sad
But to this day
A friend is a friend, that's good not bad.

Megan Tee (12)
Townley Grammar School for Girls, Bexleyheath

184

The Sound Of Thirst

This sunset painted pink and gold across parched clouds,
This sunset sung to sleep a thousand crowds.
And far beneath, a million thirsty lips,
Kissed children slipping into poverty's grips.

This moonlight whispered pleas into the skies
That hung answered in a web of lies,
And hollow promises echoed round empty wells
Mingling with the far off anguished yells
Of a mother drowning in bitter grief
Yet choking with merciless relief -
The very opposite of greed -
Of having one less mouth to feed.

This daylight brought no ray of hope -
Just more capacity to cope.
And far away, where rain fell strong,
A bursting river sang its song,
And gleaming treasure quenched the nation -
Met with nothing but frustration.
And no one thought to wonder why
It was the sky would never cry
Over lands where each drop was a jewel -
As always, the irony was cruel,
For the only drops that reached the ground,
The only water to be found,
Were the tears of the mother pouring down her cheeks
While scorched terracotta cracked and creaked
And the sun looked down from its amber throne,
And gazed at the planet it called its own.

Poppy Cozens (18)
Townley Grammar School for Girls, Bexleyheath

The Dilapidated Ground

The dare that I had accepted from Natalie has finally overcome me,
As I tentatively approached the isolated grounds behind the school,
I could feel the clouds glaring over me like a tiger standing over its prey,
The wind was wailing and screaming, to be released from its mystical spell,
But my cautious footsteps could be heard over these disruptions,
They said they would laugh at me, tease me, torture me,
If I did not do what they say,
My choices were limited,
No matter how much I refused,
My opinions were ignored,
Why? I say why?
But I daren't say it in front of Natalie and 'the girls'
They would beat me up, boy would they beat me up.
A torrent of guilt whooshed through me like a thunderstorm,
This time was meant to be for my work experience,
I couldn't believe for a second now,
I was fifteen and I was getting bullied,
I should have stayed defiant,
And told my family,
I realised that my actions conveyed the facts that I was an idiot,
I was destroying the possibilities of my success,
So I left my fear,
Left this derelict area,
And set off to improve my life so far,
I didn't care about Natalie,
Not about her jeering,
And without a second thought,
I left dilapidated grounds.

Iqra Ahmed (12)
Townley Grammar School for Girls, Bexleyheath

The Phoenix

A shifting beat of molten wings
A haunting call that slowly rings
A click of metal against stone
A beast of flame perched on its throne
Eyes shine of ruby desire
Looking out across the mire
Wings alight dry the murky mud
As temptation dares to flood
A shadow creeps behind the form
Moving colder and getting warm
A winding net is raised above
Its target a small gift for love
Wings flail as the spirit cries
Web tangled and unable to rise
Though the flames could scorch the ropes
The beast is caught from long past hopes
Once caught and never free
Was how the phoenix was meant to be?
Never dying as it returns from ash
Though this bird, it was the last.

Laura Say (16)
Townley Grammar School for Girls, Bexleyheath

You Are Here

I open my eyes,
I see you there,
You come towards me with arms spread,
You finally get to me,
Holding me tight,
You whisper something in my ear,
I don't hear because you are here,
I close my eyes,
Then open them again,
I am dreaming,
A dream that will always be in my head.

Georgina Harvey (12)
Townley Grammar School for Girls, Bexleyheath

The Vegetaball

A parsnip and a carrot, went to a ball,
where the onions made them cry
and the cucumbers were small.
The cauliflower and broccoli made friends with the Swedes,
and the potatoes came in jackets and sat with the sprouts and peas.
Then in walked the Duchess,
with King Edward and the royals from Jersey.
The runner beans thought, *that's a turnip for the books,*
and the radishes blushed, too embarrassed to look,
they squashed into the tomatoes
because there wasn't mushroom
and the beetroots went purple, boiling in the heat.
Now the vegetables are done
and I've washed off the dirt
it's time to enjoy my chocolate fudge dessert!

Katy Conybear (11)
Townley Grammar School for Girls, Bexleyheath

Guess Who?

When you're feeling pressured,
Guess who it is?
It's the 'thing' that abuses you,
The 'thing' that leaves scars on your heart
When you seek for help
It's the 'thing' that stops you again
Then it hurts you even more than before
Finally, someone reaches your distant calls
Guess who it is?
Someone kind and thoughtful
Someone who you can trust
Your scars are healing day by day
With a special person by your side
Guess who it is?
It's someone special.

Erica Cheng (12)
Townley Grammar School for Girls, Bexleyheath

Butterfly Wings

Finding a place in the burning tree
I built my cocoon on a leafless branch
There was no colour there to surround me
I could not express my feelings at all
I had made a mistake, I soon came to see
But I knew I had the power to leave this grey scene
I tore my cocoon to shreds.

I slowly unfolded my wings of liberation
Colours so bright, every known shade
I dipped and dived in the bright cyan sky
Left behind that cocoon I had foolishly made
Then I plunged to the earth where the ladybirds sang
Made my home in the swaying sea of green grass
I danced to my pounding heartbeat.

Libby Langley (13)
Townley Grammar School for Girls, Bexleyheath

Am I Dead?

I was walking down the corridor,
How will I die I thought and when will I die?
I started to get hotter and hotter and hotter,
Then I went round the corner to find my death!
There she was the girl I dreaded;
Seconds later I was on the floor,
Blood pouring out my nose, my head pounding
Am I dead? I thought.
As I got up she kicked me back down,
She called me names, oh such horrible names
I'm ridiculed for standing out, at least I'm not dead,
But it seems to me I'm her favourite game,
And I'm the one who loses,
If she'd done this hard with her fists,
At least there would be bruises.

Celine Dior (11)
Walderslade Girls' School, Chatham

Friendship

Ever since we started here,
It feels like we have throwing spears.
As I've been watching us fall and tumble,
I see our friendship erode and crumble.
I feel there's a wall that's been put in between,
We have been fighting more and getting more and more mean.
I feel like our friendship is falling apart,
Like I've been hit straight down the heart.
Oh dear friend what's happening to us,
It seems like our friendship has been hit by a bus.
It feels like our care is melting away,
But why can't our old selves just stay.
You say mean things to me but still you regret,
I've known you for 10 years which I don't want to forget.
Oh dear friend you say the meanest of words,
Instead what we got was two people hurt.
There must be something deep inside that is still there,
To be honest hurting people isn't really fair.
Could we ever get over this?
Replace this hatred with care and bliss,
Why is our friendship turned into war?
I hope it doesn't to more, more and more.
Oh why did you punch me right in the heart?
Why is this happening? This didn't happen from the start.
It feels like something is going on
What's the matter, did I do something wrong?
When there's something wrong why don't you open up?
I feel like two doors have finally been shut.
Please dear friend why are you not being kind?
Why can't you just forgive me and put this all behind?

Nicole Hobbes (11)
Walderslade Girls' School, Chatham

Sounds In My Life

The sounds I hear every day,
Are the ones I hold close,
The ones I adore the most.

The alerting of the alarm,
That wakes me when the sky is dawning,
The bubbling of the kettle,
As I have my first drink of the morning,
The crackling of my breakfast food,
Keeps my belly full,
The zipping of my skirt,
As I get ready for school.

The slamming of the car door,
As I make a short journey,
The clanking of my shoes,
As I walk on the pavement,
The zooming of cars,
As they race past me,
The swishing of the bus door,
Opening beside me.

The whispering of the children,
That surround me,
The banging of door closing,
Coming from everywhere,
The smashing of locker doors,
As people get prepared,
The siren sound,
That tells me that lesson time is near.

Katie Hood (11)
Walderslade Girls' School, Chatham

No One To Turn To

I come out of class, I'm always late
Everyone's in the cafeteria
Then I see her storming my way
Why am I her target?
Why am I her punchbag?
Her posse follow behind her
Sniggering and laughing
I know what's coming next
She holds me up to the wall
Her posse stand around her
She's so close to my face
I can feel her breath upon mine
She takes a swing
Hits me right in my gut
Her posse each have a go
Each and every one of them
I try to dodge them
But she grips me even tighter
She throws me on the ground
My shoulder makes a cracking sound
One of her gang members spits in my face
One of them turns around
And gives me a sympathetic look
I think she likes me
She wasn't as enthusiastic as the others
Oh well there's no one I can turn to
No one I can trust.

Louise Cogger (11)
Walderslade Girls' School, Chatham

The Worst Day Ever

I run into the school, my shoes untied
Deep inside I cried and cried
But on the outside I smile so weak
Soon I feel like I'm going to leak
So I run to the toilets, my eyes overflow
And then I see her and her friend Joe
I feel like I'm going to explode
But soon more tears seem to be showed
She punches me so hard I fall to the floor
Then they run out the door
I hide my face so it don't show
I never tell so no one will know
But soon I feel a fire inside
It burns and then I feel like I've took all I can earn
I burst with fury and ran out the door
I know what to do that's for sure
I hit her so hard she begins to cry
I soon get caught by Mr McLey
I'm sent to the Head, I'm in trouble
But so I lie now, I'm worth double
So this is a warning
So don't laze in the morning
Get to school on time
Don't hit because it's a crime
Just tell a person anyone will do
Just make sure this don't happen to you.

Charlotte Buck (11)
Walderslade Girls' School, Chatham

Help Me!

Now I'm the kinda shy one
always having my hair in a bun
that was the day some girls came
made up their own game
pushed me all around
especially onto the ground
calling me names was one of their
of their favourite games
time passed on
I couldn't sing a song
I couldn't sleep at night
I was in too much fright
my eyes closed
as I curled up
I had a dream
no I wasn't eating ice cream
then suddenly I knew
I was gonna make my dream come true
I told a friend
and she went round the bend
my friend didn't help
so I did it myself
and shouted, 'Help me!'

Hayley Bashford (11)
Walderslade Girls' School, Chatham

My Emotions

Today I feel happy, excited, anxious,
sad, worried, tearful, angry, mad, unhappy,
disappointed, frightened, scared, wonderful,
smiley, terrific, delighted, outstanding,
thoughtful, courageous, special, different,
in love, cautious, ashamed, shameless, tired,
bored, annoyed, dreadful, alright, sick, ill,
emotional.
These are my emotions so don't mess with them.

Jessica Dellor (11)
Walderslade Girls' School, Chatham

Depression

Depression is as cold as ice,
Depression is as dark as night,
Depression is like a tornado spiralling out of control,
Depression is not a beautiful sight,
Depression is a whirlpool of sadness,
Depression is pain and tears,
Depression is feeling like you can't breathe,
Depression is a loss of hope and fears,
Hope is the sunlight that pierces the cloud,
Hope is the seashell that whispers in your ear,
Hope is the icicle that twinkles so clear,
Hope leads to happiness,
Which makes everything worthwhile,
Like seeing the sunset,
And you can say hello to a clear, bright smile,
When you find hope and happiness,
And pull yourself out of depression,
You see all and only good things,
And the world will be your greatest possession!

Megan Standbridge (12)
Walderslade Girls' School, Chatham

Feelings At Birthday And Christmas

My birthday is soon and Christmas is near.
Which makes this my favourite time of the year.
The excitement of both is too much to handle.
I just want to blow out my birthday candle.
There is lots of excitement and happiness around.
Some of the emotions you feel -
Happy
Excited
Full of joy
Hopeful
Surprised
Worried
Anxious.

Keira-Jane King (12)
Walderslade Girls' School, Chatham

The Emotions I Feel

When I am happy the clouds will smile,
When I am sad they won't walk a mile.
When I am angry the sea crashes,
When I am being bullied the sea bashes.
When I am being taught I get a little bored,
When I am sleepy I sometimes snore.
When I am scared a volcano erupts,
When someone is bad I go 'tut-tut'
These are things that I feel
So be careful
You don't know
What will
Happen
Next.

Chelsea Chapman (11)
Walderslade Girls' School, Chatham

There's No Need For Bullying!

There is no need for bullying,
Because it only causes sadness,
There is no need for fighting,
Because it only causes pain.

Do not waste your energy,
On all this negativity,
Be positive in all you do,
And happiness will come to you.

If we could all work together,
Peace and harmony will be forever,
Protect all those that hold you dear,
No more sadness, pain or fear.

Abbie Loker-Glanville (11)
Walderslade Girls' School, Chatham

Staring New

Now I've started new
I've left my friends behind
I think about them every day
They never leave my mind.

The good memories are here
Although I'm sad and blue
We've gone our separate ways
But it's good to start a-new

We've began to grow apart
And made more new friends
We all love our new school
The fun just never ends.

Holly Wilson (11)
Walderslade Girls' School, Chatham

A Small Girl Whom I Know

Me, a small girl whom I know
So sweet, so kind and pure like snow
I know how to laugh,
I know how to cry,
I've even had to mourn,
When loved ones die.
Me, a small girl as pure as snow
Has learnt so much more than you'll ever know
I know how to get angry
I know how to get sad
But the one thing I know for sure
Is that nobody is like me!

Kimberley Haden (11)
Walderslade Girls' School, Chatham

My Sister Mia

My sister, Mia, has inspired me to be like her,
Because she is kind to everyone and never makes them frown,
She is always happy even in the morning and late at night,
She loves and cares for me and puts a smile on my face.

My sister, Mia, has inspired me to be like her,
Because she works hard and has a good job,
She has earned a lot of money and owns her own house,
My sister, Mia, has inspired me to be like her,
Because I can always trust her and she will never let me down,
I think she is a wonderful person,
I couldn't ask for a better sister.

Ellie Cufley (11)
Walderslade Girls' School, Chatham

Best Friends Forever

My friend, when I think of you,
I think of all the things that we've been through,
All the times we argued and fought,
I knew it was wrong, we sure have been taught,
I love you, dear, dear friend,
I'll write you a message and then press send,
You truly are my very best friend,
What we have, we'll keep till the end,
Friends till the end is what we will be,
Every day we'll be together, together you and me.

Emma Louise Dye (11)
Walderslade Girls' School, Chatham

Bullies

B itter taste swishes inside my mouth as she approaches
U nderneath my skin my heart pounds
L ight-headed, the world swirling
L ittle waterdrops sprinkle down my cheeks causing an
I nvasion of huge rain works
E veryone stares and laughs
S he thumped me right where it hurts in the organ I call my heart.

Jessica Sharp (11)
Walderslade Girls' School, Chatham

Intruder

How do I hate thee? Let me count the ways
I hate thee with a flamed passion, from your yellow nails
That twist and twine, to your entrance where your mood prevails.
And to the pathetic stalwart image you endeavour to portray.
I hate thee arrogant bear, your grasp you have on my mother
All is left of your love is the deadly nightshades you feed down her throat
I hate thee and wonder when you will start to make her choke
I can bear no kind words for you, nor you for me,
Only the hate we have for each other
I hate thee in a strangest way I begin to pity
As you tire and grow older you shrivel up even more
I hate thee with a hate so strong and so bold
Your weakness is my gain, not so much like before
Your minute brain aches from your heart being so cold
No one can bare your impolite ways, step father
That bring even my heart down to the floor.

Nicole Nash (16)
West Kent College, Tunbridge Wells

Nature's Cage At Our Zoo

Bars, wires and fences cage 'livestock' in
The animal: senseless?
Herbivorous, defenceless.
We built those prisons to keep our products harvesting
'Cute', 'pretty' animals - too small to cause harm,
We locked these up for self-pleasures sake,
Right and wrong? Our rules oblige to keep the calm,
Their homes *we* want for wood and land,
A state of war has rained on nature,
You scurry and run; we shall deal God's hand,
Oceans fight, their waves thrash at Man,
Yet we stab and plunge and gut its life,
'Fish don't feel pain; don't waste money on being human'
'Game' - the hunted animal now labelled 'The prey'
'Game: To play sport, to jest, to amuse oneself,'
A tragic suffering death is the game it must play,
We want to explore, we want to witness, we must see,
Shipped over and encaged an exotic beast,
A family fun trip to experience the imprisoned who were once free,
Do materials and knowledge make us God?
Does our learning and progress make us superior?
Each species ours, to poke and prod?
We would shoot the horse that would not run,
Our obese world takes little pleasure in others' laziness,
We would poison the weed that reaches for the sun,
We would put down - kill - the dog, cat, rat that nobody wants,
But who showed nature these abandoned souls?
She would curse the concrete and welcome to her abundance,
Who are we to personify nature? - She is not like us,
Separate from our want and need and eternal greed,
Focused, delirious we strangle all through our genius.

Elizabeth Bristow (18)
West Kent College, Tunbridge Wells

Untitled

How do I hate thee? Let me count the ways.
I hate thee black canvas painted red
Random splashes of paint and a meaningless unmade bed
The time I spend looking at your work are the most boring days
I hate thee waste of space in galleries your work I'd love to erase
The reason behind your work never seems to be said
I hate thee like a book with no pages it can never be read
I hate thee, you will never give other artists a chance
I hate thee, I always have from the very start
Though I am curious why you have done it, I should give it another glance
I hate thee with a hate that I could never part
I'm sure your work I could enhance
The 'artists' whom I'll never admire
I hate thee modern art.

Joanna Webb (18)
West Kent College, Tunbridge Wells

Where Were You?

Where were you at the start?
Where were you to take your part?
Where were you when your friends went to war?
Where were you when they needed more?
Where were you when the guns went off?
Where were you when the going got tough?
Where were you when they began to choke?
Where were you when their spirits broke?
Where were you when they flew over?
Where were you when they took cover?
Where were you when men started dying?
Where were you when their families were crying?
Where were you when the bombs started blowing?
Where were you when the blood started flowing?
Where were you when there was gas in the air?
Where were you? Didn't you care?

Laura Biggs (13)
Woodbridge School, Woodbridge

Young Writers Information

We hope you have enjoyed reading this
book - and that you will continue to enjoy it
in the coming years.

If you like reading and writing poetry drop
us a line, or give us a call, and we'll send
you a free information pack.

Alternatively if you would like to order further
copies of this book or any of our other titles,
then please give us a call or log onto our
website at www.youngwriters.co.uk

Young Writers Information
Remus House
Coltsfoot Drive
Peterborough
PE2 9JX
(01733) 890066